Advancing Strategic Thought Series

HUMAN INTELLIGENCE:
ALL HUMANS, ALL MINDS, ALL THE TIME

Robert D. Steele

May 2010

*****

Published by Books Express Publishing
Books Express, 2011
ISBN 978-1-780395-22-4

Books Express publications are available from all good retail and online booksellers. For
publishing proposals and direct ordering please contact us at: info@books-express.com

2. *The New Craft of Intelligence: Achieving Asymmetric Advantage in the Face of Nontraditional Threats*, February 2002, available from *www.strategicstudiesinstitute.army.mil/pubs/display.cfm?pub ID=217*. This monograph is the third in the Strategic Studies Institute's "Studies in Asymmetry" Series. In it, the author examines two paradigm shifts — one in relation to the threat and a second in relation to intelligence methods — while offering new models for threat analysis and intelligence operations in support of policy, acquisition, and commands engaged in nontraditional asymmetric confrontation.

3. Chapter 9, "Threats, Strategy and Force Structure: An Alternative Paradigm for National Security in the 21st Century," in Steven Metz, ed., *Revising the Two MTW Force-Shaping Paradigm*, Carlisle, PA: Strategic Studies Institute, U.S. Army War College, April 2001, pp. 139-163, available from *www.strategicstudiesinstitute.army.mil/pdffiles/ PUB297.pdf.*

4. Chapter 12, "Presidential Leadership and National Security Policymaking," in Douglas T. Stuart, ed., *Organizing for National Security*, Carlisle, PA: Strategic Studies Institute, U.S. Army War College, November 2000, pp. 245-282, available from *www. strategicstudiesinstitute.army.mil/pdffiles/PUB299.pdf.*

FOREWORD

For almost 2 decades, the author has been exploring the opportunities for strategy, force structure, and interagency or coalition operations in light of changes in the real world. His first monograph, *The New Craft of Intelligence: Achieving Asymmetric Advantage in the Face of Nontraditional Threats*, outlined the relevance of his vision to asymmetric warfare, and has since been proven to be true. His second monograph, *Information Operations: Putting the "I" Back Into DIME*, established the technical, conceptual, and doctrinal opportunities for a world in which every soldier's primary duty is not to be a rifleman (an inherent responsibility), but rather to apply the wisdom of Colonel John Boyd, USAF (Ret.), and Observe, Orient, Decide, and Act (OODA) — to be, at all times, a consummate collector, producer, consumer, and analyst of real-world real-time information and intelligence, while also serving as a communicator at a face-to-face level.

With this third and final monograph in the series, the author explores the centrality of Human Intelligence (HUMINT) in meeting the needs of the U.S. Army, as well as the Department of Defense (DoD), and the whole of government, for relevant information and tailored intelligence essential to creating a national security strategy; for defining whole of government policies that work in harmony; for acquisition of the right capabilities at the right price in time to be useful; and for operations, both local and global.

The author outlines 15 distinct types of HUMINT, only four of which are classified (defensive and offensive counterintelligence, clandestine operations, and covert action), with the other 11 being predominantly unclassified. Additionally, he argues that they are completely lacking in integrated management or innovative leadership. The author, well-grounded in the literature of how complex organizations fail and how resilience and sustainability can be achieved through collective intelligence, offers the U.S. Army an orientation to a world in which thinkers displace shooters as the center of gravity for planning, programming, and budgeting, as well as the proper structuring of mission mandates, force structures, and tactics and techniques to be used in any given mission area.

DOUGLAS C. LOVELACE, JR.
Director
Strategic Studies Institute

ABOUT THE AUTHOR

ROBERT D. STEELE is a retired Marine Corps infantry and intelligence officer and also qualified as an S-1/Adjutant, with service at all levels from platoon to Service Headquarters. After four years active duty, the balance of twenty to be spent in the Individual Ready Reserve (IRR), and a decade as a clandestine case officer for the Central Intelligence Agency (CIA), he resigned from the CIA to accept a Marine Corps invitation to be the senior civilian responsible for creating the Marine Corps Intelligence Center (today a Command) and served as the study director for the flagship study, *Overview of Planning and Programming Factors for Expeditionary Operations in the Third World.* He resigned from the Marine Corps civil service in 1993 to lead the modern Open Source Intelligence (OSINT) revolution, and is the author of the DIA, NATO, and SOF OSINT Handbooks, as well as personally responsible for training 7,500 officers from 66 countries. His latest book, *INTELLIGENCE for EARTH: Clarity, Diversity, Integrity, and Sustainability*, outlines a course of action for creating public intelligence in the public interest across all organizations, beginning with the United Nations. Mr. Steele founded OSS.Net, Inc. and Earth Intelligence Network, the latter a 501c3 public charity, and is the foremost proponent for a Swedish concept enhancing, Multinational, Multiagency, Multidisciplinary, Multi-domain Information-Sharing and Sense-Making (M4IS2). Mr. Steele holds graduate degrees in international relations and public administration from Lehigh University and the University of Oklahoma. He has also earned certificates in intelligence policy from Harvard University and a diploma in defense studies from the Naval War College.

PREFACE

This monograph was inspired by three U.S. Army encounters. First, was a *pro bono* engagement with the new U.S. Army Civil Affairs Brigade, then commanded by Col Ferd Irizarry, USA. His vision for the future is breathtaking: a future in which Civil Affairs personnel are the essential facilitators for transitions to and from hostilities, as well as the essential means by which multinational information-sharing and sense-making that is unclassified, can be shared, and helps to prevent conflict while creating local stabilizing wealth. Next came the annual U.S. Army Strategy Conference of 2008, focused on "Rebalancing the Instruments of National Power." The findings of that event are a perfect introduction for this monograph, and are summarized in an Appendix with pointers to longer summaries. Finally came an encounter with a most professional officer, the Chief of Staff for the Directorate for Human Intelligence (DH) within the Defense Intelligence Agency (DIA). That individual's open-mindedness led to an overnight drafting of the new craft of human intelligence (HUMINT) in the context of the DIA's global mission and global challenges.

My own view, formed over 3 decades in government service, is that the military is the one part of government that is able to move, do, and communicate on a global basis, and we need to find a way to expand that capability to empower the "whole of government." I believe that the Department of Defense (DoD) must become a "core force" for the nation, a broader deeper foundation for national security than merely warfighting, with two major support functions:

    1. Be the basis for a coherent polity, using a uni-

versal draft with three options after a common boot camp: Armed Forces, Peace Corps, or Homeland Service.

2. Be the global general service for multinational and interagency communications, intelligence, logistics, and mobility.

From Base Force to Core Force and Beyond.

General Colin Powell, USA (Ret.), devised the concept of a "Base Force." This inspired me, when invited to speak in Germany at the George Marshall Center in the 1990s, to devise the concept of the "Core Force." Within DoD, the U.S. Army would be the "core of the core" (see Figure 1.)

Core Force for Peace

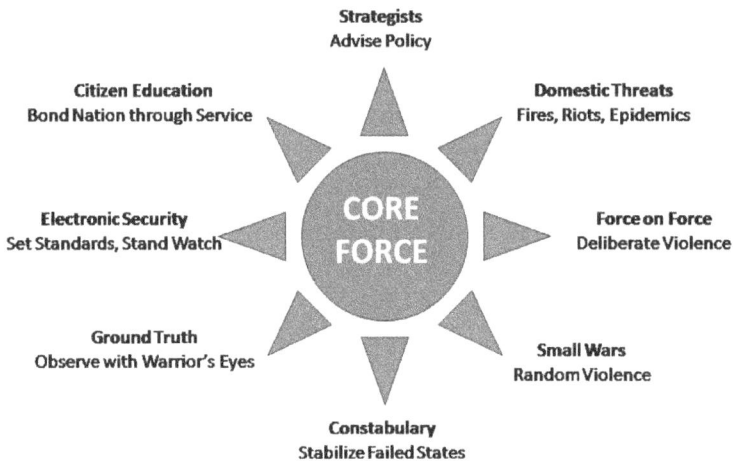

Strategists
Advise Policy

Citizen Education
Bond Nation through Service

Domestic Threats
Fires, Riots, Epidemics

Electronic Security
Set Standards, Stand Watch

CORE
FORCE

Force on Force
Deliberate Violence

Ground Truth
Observe with Warrior's Eyes

Small Wars
Random Violence

Constabulary
Stabilize Failed States

Figure 1: Core Force with Eight Human Functions.

The core force, the inner circle, represents the services of common concern without which no world power can operate: the ability to communicate anywhere, anytime; the ability to acquire and make sense of information so as to produce decision support (96 percent unclassified and shareable); and the ability to move personnel and materials from any point to any point in a most expeditious manner, with desolate airfields unsuitable for commercial aviation being the norm. We can reconfigure our combatant commands as whole of government task forces, with the appropriate assistant secretaries moving their flags into the field.

The eight human functions represent the value-added areas where the military is uniquely qualified and competent as the primary element of government around which we can all rally.

At the very top is strategic thinking and advice to policymakers, with one big difference: the military — at every rank — must make speaking truth to power vastly more important to its ethos than loyalty to the chain of command. The Constitution is what we swear to support in our Oath of Office, not the chain of command. Truth and morality are a primary force.

Next down are two critical domestic roles: bonding our citizenry (including immigrants regardless of age) through common training and service; and being able to address domestic challenges with military discipline and effectiveness. I am among those who believe that the National Guard should revert to being primarily a homeland force, and one focused on localized disaster relief and the maintenance of good order and discipline in times of crisis, while also available for short duration (no more than 90 days) missions to aid others outside the United States.

Electronic security and ground truth are global missions that require a degree of pervasive defense presence in cyberspace on the one hand, and a degree of pervasive but inoffensive presence—real humans with human eyes, ears, and brains—everywhere. We have failed at both, in part because we spent too much time on offensive electronic warfare, something the Chinese have mastered, and not enough time on establishing standards that protect all electronic information, not just sensitive information.

Of all the missions depicted in Figure 1, none is more important than the ground truth mission. The reality is that our embassies have become little fortresses from which few dare to venture far afield. The diplomats are in the minority within their own embassy, and have virtually no funds for entertaining diverse constituencies, and even less for commissioning local commercial sources of legal, and ethical information for specific products. Indeed, the only people with money to spend in the U.S. overseas community are the spies, and they insist that one commit treason before they will listen. In combination, how we relate to the rest of the world is pathologically inept.[1]

Force on force, and constabulary operations or small wars, are two completely different endeavors in every possible sense of the word, and require two completely distinct forces that train, equip, and organize for their assigned mission. The two do not overlap and cannot be mixed. They can be orchestrated in those instances where one front is conventional and the other unconventional, but they are not interchangeable forces.

Where does this leave us? Here are the high points:

1. Unclassified decision support — ground truth — is the single most valuable and relevant service the U.S. Army can provide to the rest of the DoD and the rest of the government as well as the nation (schoolhouses, chambers

of commerce, etc.). Unclassified ground truth is not the purview of the spies—they have rejected that mission, leaving the way open for the Civil Affairs community to become the ombudsmen of the best truth outside the wire.

2. Peer-to-peer human communication and interaction is the single most valuable aspect of a global presence. General Anthony Zinni, USMC (Ret.), is on record as emphasizing the importance of long-term relationships and of truly understanding the character and nature of those with whom one is dealing.[2] In this vein, the Army Strategy Conference of 2008 placed equal emphasis on the human terrain system (HTS) and on having a corps of advisors who are resident in their respective countries, not simply going in and out as mobile training teams (MTT).

3. The importance of deep cultural knowledge cannot be overstated. Cultural Intelligence is a key factor in preventing conflict as in stabilizing and reconstructing areas torn by conflict.[3]

4. Peaceful preventive measures, as called for by General Al Gray, USMC (Ret.), then Commandant of the Marine Corps, are a primary mission of the U.S. Army, no longer an afterthought or an unfunded deficiency. Civil Affairs, not the tank corps or artillery or even the infantry, is the king of the 21st century battlefield. Real men *prevent* war; and if not, achieve "one man—one bullet" precision as needed

The U.S. Army, the DoD, and the Republic.

America is at a crossroads. The lack of an integrated interagency process for developing coherent sustainable (affordable and realistic) strategy is at a historic low point. We are unwisely spending $75 billion a year on global secret technical collection efforts, while spending relatively nothing on processing, or interagency sharing of data, or on decision support. This is the root cause for our inability to plan, program, and budget for whole of government strategy and operations.[4]

This monograph aspires to be nothing less than a manifesto for mental and cultural transformation of the U.S. Army, the U.S. DoD, all civilian elements of our national security bureaucracy, and all external organizations such as international organizations (IO) and nongovernmental organizations (NGOs) as well as foundations. The core concept within this monograph is that the U.S. Army can:

1. Be the first within the U.S. Government to understand — as the Singapore military understood instantly — that we must defend America against *all* threats, not just nation-state military threats.

2. Be the first within the U.S. Government to understand — as corporations are now rapidly appreciating — that Generation 2.0 is the first generation of young people who are not "little versions of us." They are digital natives; they have transformed themselves in the process of growing up, and most (not all) of our tried and true boot camp processes are history.

3. Be the first within the U.S. Government to understand that decision support information (intelligence regardless of classification) is the key to creating and stabilizing the earth.

The greatest strategic error we have made has been to neglect the education and the civic engagement of our public, a public that has grown out of touch with global realities, less competitive in the international marketplace, and virtually oblivious to the corporate, federal, state, and local miss-steps enacted in our name. Information costs money and confuses; public intelligence makes money, guides money, and can create a prosperous world at peace.

The U.S. Army can combine an appreciation of external reality and a valuation of our digital natives by becoming the brain group for global interagency and combined operations that leverage information peace-keeping.

Figure 2 summarizes the relevance of this work to each of the Army's strategic issues.

Global War on Terrorism	Understanding, confronting, altering evil belief systems; Strategic communications as behavior and budget; reality-based metrics.
Homeland Security	Cannot have a smart Army built on a dumb population. Need to build a smart nation.
Regional	Systematic outreach at every level down to neighborhoods, clans, and tribes.
Military Change	Must train, equip, and organize interagency and coalition teams with gendarme and other soft-power intelligence and operations.
Strategy	Only reality-based comprehensive strategy will have a chance. Cannot keep Navy and Air Force shares of the budget constant.
Landpower	Landpower is about mind on mind, not machine on machine, or even man on man.
Landpower Generation and Sustainment	Army must adapt to embrace digital natives, and learn how to extend free education and training to multinational multiagency forces.
Leadership, Personnel Management, and Culture	Everything has changed. Information operations are 80% of the leadership challenge — must learn Way of the Wiki, bottom up, adjust budgets.
War and Society	We are in a total war forever, 24/7, all information, all languages.

Figure 2. Relevance to Army Strategic Issues.

This monograph specifically recommends the immediate conversion of the Coalition Coordination Center (CCC) at the U.S. Central Command (USCENTCOM) into a Multinational Decision Support Center (MDSC) capable of early warning, predictive analysis, and unclassified decision support to stabilization, reconstruction, humanitarian assistance, and disaster relief operations. Under the oversight of the Director of the DIA, this capability could be offered to the United Nations (UN) and other NGOs as a means of better implementing the recommendations of the Defense Science Board study on *Transitions to and from Hostilities*.[5] Most significantly, this would also provide a neutral multinational hub for receiving the bulk of the global information needed to make sense of the world, a hub that is not now available to the secret national intelligence community of any nation; and it would simultaneously serve as a foundation for harmonizing government, corporate, non-governmental, and charitable spending on assistance to all underdeveloped and/or unstable areas.

This work, in support of the Strategic Studies Institute, the U.S. Army War College, and the Army's strategic issues, provides a review of the nuts and bolts of Seventh Generation Warfare (see Figure 3), a level of warfare previously referred to as "Information Peacekeeping," the logical follow-on to the six generations of warfare so ably studied and taught by Dr. Max Manwaring, U.S. Army (Ret.), of the Strategic Studies Institute.[6]

Warfare Era	What Do We Need to Know?
1st Generation	Easy: Where is the army?
2nd Generation	Easy: Where are the trenches?
3rd Generation	Moderate: How many with what?
4th Generation	Hard: Watch every non-state actor.
5th Generation	Hard: Watch everything on the fly.
6th Generation	Hard: Make sense of billions of bits.
7th Generation	Very Hard: 24/7, 183 languages, and put our own strategy, policy, structure, and budget in order.

Figure 3. War and Peace: The Seventh Generation.

In Sun Tzu's terms, it is safe to say that today he would suggest that we do not know our enemy, we do not know ourselves, and we are thus at very high risk of failure.[7] More recent books examining the collapse of complex societies arrive at a similar supporting conclusion: When governments fail to adapt, to have open minds and receive reality-based information, and when they persist in policies, behaviors, and investments that are out of touch with reality, then they tend to lose legitimacy, as well as efficacy, and secessionist movements repressed in the past tend to come to the fore. Most interestingly, secessionist movements succeed in their objective primarily when the nation they seek to separate from is engaged in arduous combat on a large scale, far from the homeland.[8] In the information age, the age of globalization, and the age of the five billion people at the bottom of the human pyramid, there are no longer enough guns to force any decision on any population.[9] Stabilization, reconstruction, and a new form of engaged democracy, combined with moral capitalism, orchestrated giving, and a heavy blend of sustained cultural awareness, education, and humanitarian operations, are going to be the primary instruments of interagency and coalition forces if we are to achieve a sustainable peace in this century.

In this environment, as in the law enforcement environment, shooting is the *last* thing we want a Soldier to do, and thinking is the *only* thing we will want every Soldier to be doing 24/7. In this context:

- **Consensus** replaces command,
- **Education** replaces discipline,
- **Information operations** evolve to demand greater budget and manpower share—no more than 10 percent of it secret,
- **Multinational** replaces unilateral,
- **Research**—multinational research—replaces unilateral acquisition, and sharing replaces hoarding,
- **Soft power** displaces hard power,
- **Funding emphasis** shifts from complex heavy metal weapons, to multinational open sources, shared decision support, and full spectrum peace operations,
- **Training** emphasizes multicultural, multiagency, multidisciplinary, and multidomain information sharing and sense-making (M4IS2).

The best concise explanation of the importance of the radical departures from tradtional command, communication, education, information operations, intelligence, and research and training is to offer two competing viewpoints of what the primary role of every Army or other service person is (1) *Every Soldier will be a rifleman*; or (2) *Every Soldier will be a collector, consumer, producer, and provider of information and intelligence.*

Digital Natives.

A major challenge facing the U.S. Army is the changing nature of its population, both officer and enlisted. Figure 4 summarizes the competing—the starkly distinct—natures of the population entering on duty (learners) and the population now in command and control (teachers).

Digital Native Learners	Digital Native Teachers
Prefer receiving information quickly from multiple multimedia sources	Prefer slow and controlled release of information from limited sources
Prefer parallel processing and multitasking	Prefer singular processing and single or limited tasking
Prefer processing pictures, sources, and video before text	Prefer to provide text before pictures, sounds and video
Prefer random access to hyperlinked multimedia information	Prefer to provide information linearly, logically and sequentially
Prefer to interact/network simultaneously with many others	Prefer students to work independently rather than network and interact
Prefer to learn "just in time"	Prefer to teach "just in case" (it's on the exam)
Prefer instant gratification and instant rewards	Prefer deferred gratification and deferred rewards
Prefer learning that is relevant, instantly useful and fun	Prefer to teach to the curriculum guide and standardized tests

Figure 4. Differences Between Incoming and Commanding Populations.[10]

At its most fundamental, seventh generation warfare is total, pervasive, sustained, nuanced, and can only be won by fighting ideas, not weapons.[11] Soldiers must be *both* first to fight *and* fighting smart.

Sun Tsu had it right. To defeat the enemy without fighting is the acme of a warrior's skill.[12] We have wasted 50 years and destroyed tens of millions of lives, eradicating entire cultures, because we failed to heed President and General Dwight D. Eisenhower's warning about the military-industrial complex, and because our flag officers have forgotten their Oaths of Commission and confused loyalty to partisan politicians, with their responsibility to respect the integrity of the Constutition and always—without exception—tell the truth, the whole truth, and nothing but the truth. The plague of falsified reporting, including operational test and readiness reporting and casualty reporting, as well as suicide statistics, is a disgrace to the heritage of West Point's "Long Gray Line," and to its famous motto, Duty, *Honor,* Country.[13]

Brainpower, not Firepower, is what we need to bring to bear, and we need to do this 24/7 in all languages and all mediums.[14] It is in that context that this monograph reinventing HUMINT is respectfully presented to the U.S. Army.

ENDNOTES

1. My second graduate thesis, for the University of Oklahoma, studies strategic and tactical information management for national security, using the three embassies I was familiar with, to draw out an understanding of what information we have access to, exploit, share, and make sense of. The conclusion of the study was that embassies access 20 percent of what can be known that is relevant, and in the process of communicating back to Washington, mostly via hard copy in the diplomatic pouch, spill 80 percent of that. Hence, Washington is operating on 2 percent of the available relevant information.

2. He makes this point in Tom Clancy, General Tony Zinni, USMA (Ret.) and Tony Koltz, *Battle Ready,* Berkeley, CA: Berkley

Trade, 2005; and also in General Tony Zinni, USMA (Ret.) and Tony Koltz, *The Battle for Peace*, New York: Palgrave McMillan, 2007.

3. I consider this topic (Cultural Intelligence) to be so important that I have scheduled a book on *Cultural Intelligence: Faith, Ideology, & the Five Minds for Peace* for 2009. The editors will be Dr. Susan Cannon, whose degree is in Integral Consciousness, and Professor Daniel Berghart, of the National Defense Intelligence College, among a handful of U.S. Government officers with a deep grasp of this vital topic. Existing references include Jean-Marie Bonthous, "Culture: The Missing Intelligence Variable," presented to the annual international conference of Open Source Intelligence, 1993, available from *www.phibetaiota.net/?p=4195*; my own "Information Peacekeeping & The Future of Intelligence: The United Nations, Smart Mobs, & the Seven Tribes," available from *www.phibetaiota.net/?p=2823*; and more recently, John P. Coles, "Incorporating Cultural Intelligence into Joint Doctrine," *IOSphere*, Spring 2006. Given the fact that most intelligence analysts have been on the job less than 5 years and have virtually no understanding of foreign languages, cultures, and environments, I consider this the single greatest challenge facing the U.S. Government in the 21st century. Within the public literature, one finds two aspects of cultural intelligence: one focused on *cultural imperialism*, the other on *cultural intelligence* as a facilitator of commercial transactions. It merits comment that there is an entire literature on "client relationships" that can be translated to meet U.S. Army needs. Ross Dawson's *Developing Knowledge-Based Client Relationships: The Future of Professional Services*, Maryland Heights, MO: Butterworth-Heineman, 2000, is representative.

4. The 7-year mark is from the UN and scientific reporting that says that we reach an irreversible tipping point with respect to climate change and global warming within 7 years. The longer mark is one I have assigned, during which I believe the United States, and the U.S. Army and its Civil Affairs Brigade in particular, must pursue peace on all fronts, using shared information and unclassified decision support—including the Earth-Game™—as the common language of peace.

5. Defense Science Board, *Transition to and From Hostilities*, Washington, DC: Office of the Undersecretary of Defense for Acquisition, Technology, and Logistics, January 2005. This report, and a second report done in the same year on *Strategic Communication*, comprise the foundation for a renaissance of irregular warfare, including what General Peter Schoomaker called "White Hat SOF" and what General Al Gray, then Commandant of the Marine Corps, called "peaceful preventive measures." General Gray's article on "Intelligence Challenges in the 1990s," *American Intelligence Journal*, Winter 1988-89, remains a seminal work and is available from *www.oss.net/BASIC*.

6. Max G. Manwaring, as briefed to the international conference on open source intelligence, "War and Conflict: Six Generations," 2003.

7. Chinese philosopher and General Sun Tzu's famous aphorism, "If you know your enemies and know yourself, you can win a hundred battles without a single loss," is available from *en.wikipedia.org/wiki/The Art.of.War#Quotations*.

8. See Joseph Tainter, *The Collapse of Complex Societies*, Cambridge, UK: Cambridge University Press, 1990; and Peter Turchin, *War and Peace and War: The Rise and Fall of Empires*, New York: Plume, 2007.

9. This point is capably made by Jonathan Schell, *The Unconquerable World: Power, Nonviolence, and the Will of the People*, New York: Penguin, 2005. I am not opposed to the use of force, but believe that it has become an ineffective tool for achieving political ends. On this pragmatic basis, Schell builds a case for civil noncooperation, which he argues has long played a crucial role in deciding otherwise bloody conflicts.

10. Charles Babuti Murphy, Apple Education, available from *www.apple.com/au/education/digitalkids/disconnect/landscape.html*.

11. This idea is illustrated in the movie *War Games,* which climaxes with the computer being taught that the only winning solution is to not compete. There is a wealth of literature that supports the proposition that the politics of secrecy and scarcity

have inflicted unnecessary suffering on hundreds of millions. Corruption, both within governments and within corporations that have created a global class war, has led to the annual expenditure of over $900 billion a year on war, when informed calculations suggest that for less than a third of that, $230 billion a year, we can eradicate all 10 of the high-level threats. An early overview by Australian Lieutenant Colonel Ian Wing, "Broadened Concepts of Security Operations," *Strategic Forum*, National Defense University, #148, October 1998, available from *www.ndu.edu/inss/strforum/SF148/forum148.html*, provides a helpful listing of peace-related mission areas.

12. Sun Tzu.

13. Falsified reporting is best known at the acquisition level. Two examples include the Marine Corps squadron commander falsifying reports on the VS-22 operational test and evaluation performance, and the U.S. Army's National Ground Intelligence Center (NGIC) falsifying data to justify desired weapon systems procurements. See "Marine Fired After Being Accused of Falsifying Osprey Records," Knight Ridder/Tribune News Service, January 18, 2001; and Sherrie Gossett, "Intel Allegedly Falsified to Justify Weapons Purchases," CNSNews.com Staff, March 16, 2006. The lack of an independent Operational Test & Evaluation Agency (OTEA) has been a back-burner issue since Chuck Spinney made the cover of *TIME* in the 1980s as a whistleblower. The author is personally familiar with Marine Corps deception, for example, parking all vehicles on the dock when they arrive, so as to keep them in C-2 status, knowing that to use them would be to break them.

14. The good news is that *Public Intelligence* in six slices is here to stay: *Collective* (social networks), *Peace* (harmonization of peaceful preventive measures), *Commercial* (from moral green to golden peace), *Gift* (harmonization of charitable giving against the 10 high-level threats), *Cultural* (raising a new generation without embedded biases), and *Earth Intelligence* (eliminating the human consumption of the Earth) are ascendant.

HUMAN INTELLIGENCE (HUMINT): ALL HUMANS, ALL MINDS, ALL THE TIME

INTRODUCTION

Human intelligence (HUMINT) has been moribund in the United States since the 1970s, if not earlier, as the U.S. rushed to substitute technology for thinking (intelligence producers) and partisanship for discourse (intelligence consumers). Persons involved in counterintelligence (CI), security, analysis, and intelligence consumation are included in my definition of HUMINT. Over the course of several decades, we have destroyed clandestine HUMINT, while also neglecting CI and security, depreciating open source intelligence (OSINT)[1]— which comprises 80 percent[2] of the harvestable foundation for HUMINT—and ignoring the educational needs of our Soldiers,[3] analysts, and our consumers.

Today it can reasonably be argued that only the U.S. President receives decision support (mediocre at best) from a $75 billion a year U.S. Intelligence Community (USIC),[4] while cabinet officials and congressional committees receive none at all. Defense officials receive 4 percent, at best[5] of what they need to know from secret sources and methods, little of that useful to the *Quadrennial Defense Review* (QDR) or other whole of government planning.

In this monograph, I focus only on HUMINT as a broad multidisciplinary endeavor, not on known USIC deficiencies or global data pathologies and information asymmetries not yet addressed by the USIC or the U.S. Government (USG) as a whole. HUMINT is defined as 15 distinct subdisciplinary specializations,[6] all of which must be managed as a whole in order to enable cross-fertilization among overt, covert, and clandestine sources and methods.

I conclude that, in light of the lack of a whole of government decision support architecture, and the clear and present danger associated with the 10 high-level threats to humanity, eight of which are nonmilitary, the Department of Defense (DoD) is the only element of the USG able to create a 21st century HUMINT capability—a "Smart Nation."[7]

THREATS, STRATEGY, FORCE STRUCTURE, AND ACTION-SPENDING PLANS

The USG is supposed to be attending to all threats to humanity and the nation by devising a strategy and attendant force structure (capabilities) for each element of whole of government operations. The tax-payer funds are the *means*, the government is the *ways*, and a prosperous world at peace is supposed to be the *end*.

I have come to the conclusion that intelligence without strategy, intelligence without good governance, is inherently wasteful, fraudulent, and abusive. This compounds the waste, fraud, and abuse that is the current condition of 60 percent of the USG—and 80 percent of the USIC—today.[8]

Implicit in this is the kernel of an idea, that defense intelligence, no matter how ably it might be conceptualized, developed, and implemented, is itself fruitless in the absence of good governance and holistic whole of government operations. The current Secretary of Defense has alluded to this in his statement that "the military cannot do it alone."[9] This is correct, but it avoids the underlying problem: We have a government that is inherently incoherent and incapable.

The USG ignores 8 of the 10 threats to humanity: (1) poverty, (2) infectious disease, (3) environmental degradation, (4) interstate conflict, (5) civil war, (6) genocide, (7) other atrocities, (8) proliferation, (9) terrorism, and (10) transnational crime.[10] The cabinet departments receive no intelligence (decision support) of note from the secret USIC, and are inept at creating their own unclassified decision support—they actually represent the *recipients* of taxpayer largesse, not the public interest or even less the taxpayers themselves. This places the burden on the DoD and the U.S. Army.

The President—like all others in our government—is a good person trapped in a bad system. Neither the National Security Council (NSC) nor the Office of Management and Budget (OMB), nor the Congress of the United States with its varied staff elements, including the generally superb Government Accountability Office (GAO), are capable of serving the public interest for one simple reason: We are a "dumb" nation in which the taxpayers have abdicated their civic duty to attend to government, demand a return on investment (ROI) for their taxes, and exercise their responsibility to *be* the sovereign Republic that the government *serves*.

A NATION'S BEST DEFENSE

From 1988 onwards, inspired by all that I learned as a co-founder of the Marine Corps Intelligence Agency (MCIA), today a command, I have sought to reform national intelligence, now on the tail end of the second of three eras.[11] The first era, the era of secret war and ostensibly deniable covert actions tantamount to undeclared war, ended with the 1986 U.S. conviction in the World Court for mining the harbors of Nicaragua.[12] The second era, the era of strategic analysis fostered by Sherman Kent in the aftermath of World War II, lost the last of its integrity in the Vietnam war, when "reasonable dishonesty" and the politicization of analysis castrated the Central Intelligence Agency (CIA). The CIA has become a gulag,[13] *both* because it lost its integrity, *and* because it failed to get a grip on openly-available information.[14]

The 1980s were an *interregnum*, and as one of the first officers to be assigned terrorism as a primary target, I can testify that we were not serious then, and I do not believe we are serious now — not because we do not try, but because we do not understand the system-of-systems approach to waging peace alongside irregular warfare.[15]

Today the public is discovering that its elected and appointed leaders lack the depth and breadth of understanding — or the intelligence (decision support) — to make sense of and address the 10 high-level threats to humanity. Our leaders to date have been incapable of or unwilling to harmonize the 12 core policies[16] within our own government (to include production of a sustainable balanced budget), and also appear oblivious to the impending collapse of an overly complex top-down governance structure that has failed to adapt and is in no way anticipatory, coherent, resilient, or sustainable.

There *is* good news. The related concepts of Open Source Intelligence (OSINT), bottom-up collective intelligence, and the social creation of infinite wealth are emergent. It is in this context that I believe we will see a rebirth of the intelligence profession. We are at the very beginning of a new era of smart nations, clever continents, and the world brain complemented by an EarthGame™ in which all humans have access to all information in all languages all the time. The time has come to sharply redirect national and defense intelligence. I suggest we begin with HUMINT,[17] and that we redefine it as being comprised of education, intelligence, and research, with the citizen (and the Soldier in the field) as the prime factor.

This may not seem important to the U.S. Army at first glance, but it is, because bad decisions made in isolation from the totality of our national interests (e.g., surging in Afghanistan being treated as an isolated decision without regard to the state of the economy or of the treasury) ultimately lead to the U.S. Army being put way out on a limb.

"A Nation's best defense is an educated citizenry."[18] *Humanity Ascending is the mission, HUMINT is the foundation. This is as true for the U.S. Army as it is for the Republic as a whole.*

HUMINT FOR THE PRESIDENT

In 1994, I conceptualized the end of the linear paradigm of intelligence, and the emergence of the diamond paradigm.[19] (See Figure 1.)

LINEAR PARADIGM   **DIAMOND PARADIGM**

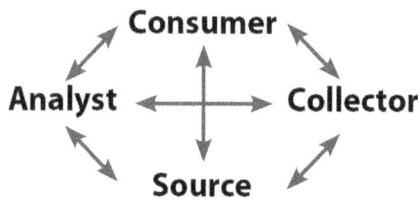

Consumer
↓ ↑
Analyst
↓ ↑
Collector
↓ ↑
Source

Consumer
Analyst ←→ Collector
Source

Figure 1. Linear versus Diamond Intelligence Process.

The linear process is what we still have in place today, and "intelligence" is placed before the President just once a day, in a largely sterile "President's Daily Brief" (PDB). Intelligence is *not* at his side throughout the day. Now imagine a completely new process in which the President (or whatever "decider" is being served) is exposed to the complete range of all human knowledge in all languages, most of it not secret and shareable, as needed. The construct shown in Figure 2 is equally applicable for every policymaker in the DoD, for every acquisition manager, for every commander, for every staff action officer all the way to every Special Forces A Team commander or company commander in the field.

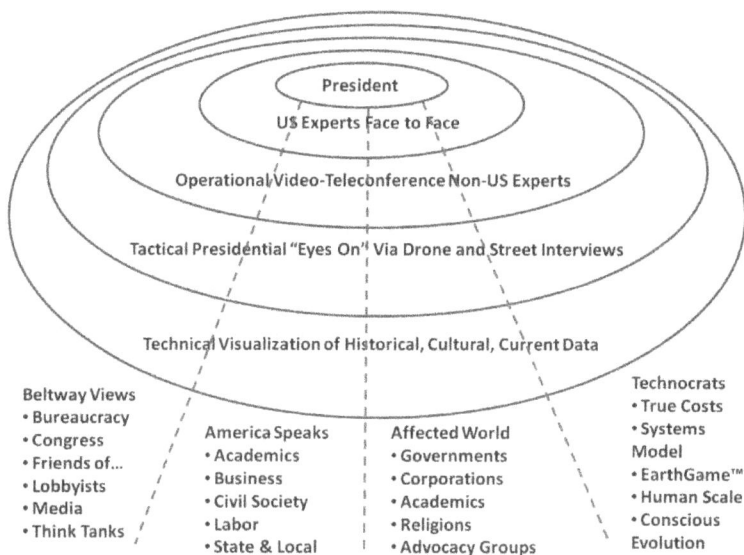

President

US Experts Face to Face

Operational Video-Teleconference Non-US Experts

Tactical Presidential "Eyes On" Via Drone and Street Interviews

Technical Visualization of Historical, Cultural, Current Data

Beltway Views
• Bureaucracy
• Congress
• Friends of...
• Lobbyists
• Media
• Think Tanks

America Speaks
• Academics
• Business
• Civil Society
• Labor
• State & Local

Affected World
• Governments
• Corporations
• Academics
• Religions
• Advocacy Groups

Technocrats
• True Costs
• Systems Model
• EarthGame™
• Human Scale
• Conscious Evolution

Figure 2. Putting the President in Touch with Humanity and Reality.

HUMINT FOR THE SECRETARY

When General Alfred M. Gray, USMC, then Commandant of the Marine Corps (CMC) directed the creation of what became the MCIA in the early 1980s, he was driven by the same vision that led to the creation of the Marine Corps University: no one else—not the U.S. Navy, not the U.S. Army, not the U.S. Air Force—was properly and fully addressing the needs of the nation's only combined arms expeditionary force. Each of the other services developed policies, acquisition programs, and operational campaign plans based on being the biggest with the mostest, with ample time to deploy and no worries about logistics supportability. My mission, as the senior civilian, was to create a center that would meet the commandant's needs for intelligence support for policy, for acquisition (both requirements for and countermeasures against), and only tangentially, to also support the Fleet Marine Force (FMF), that was in theory adequately supported by the new consolidated Joint Intelligence Centers (JIC) within each theater.

The fact that there was literally nothing at all in the secret databases about 80 percent of the world—the 80 percent where the Marines almost always went—and that no one at any level had access to open sources of information in 183 languages, most of it not online (still true today), only became clear after we spent the first $20 million.

As the Secretary of Defense seeks to address the "Valley of Death" in defense acquisition,[20] along with the continuing recalcitrance of the three big Services reluctant to risk budget share,[21] he would do well to remember Howard Odum's counsel on the need to understand (and I would add, influence) the system of which one is a part.[22] Put bluntly, not only can the military not "do it alone," which the Secretary recognizes, the military also cannot succeed in the future unless we first restructure and rebalance all of the instruments of national power.[23]

Absent a complete makeover of national and defense intelligence as well as defense engineering, DoD will continue to operate in the context of a pathologically deficient policymaking environment divorced from holistic reality; a 1950s government structure that is severely deficient in every respect, beginning with a stovepiped planning, programming, and budgeting system (PPBS); and an international spectrum of players (what I call the "eight tribes")[24] that is seeking leadership — intellectual and intelligence leadership or decision support — on how to create a prosperous world at peace.[25]

The Secretary is overlooking the actionable truth right under his nose: Until he asks the right question, he will continue to get the wrong answer.[26]

THE FAILURE OF HUMINT (STOVEPIPES, SEGREGATION, AND SECRECY)

Max Weber is renowned for his theory of bureaucracy, a model or system for controlling people, things, and most importantly, information. Under this theory, "lanes in the road" or "stovepipes" become sacrosanct fiefdoms. Under this theory, applied in the academic world, specialization leads to segregation, and segregation ultimately leads to stupidity — ignorance of the whole, and even ignorance of the role the special element plays in the whole.[27]

Put differently, the entire body of human knowledge has been misdirected toward reductionism, knowing more and more about less and less, to the point that no one has the whole picture. Former Secretary of Defense Donald Rumsfeld made this criticism of the classified world with respect to its knowledge of missile defense intelligence; it is even more true of all unclassified knowledge.[28] (See Figure 3.)

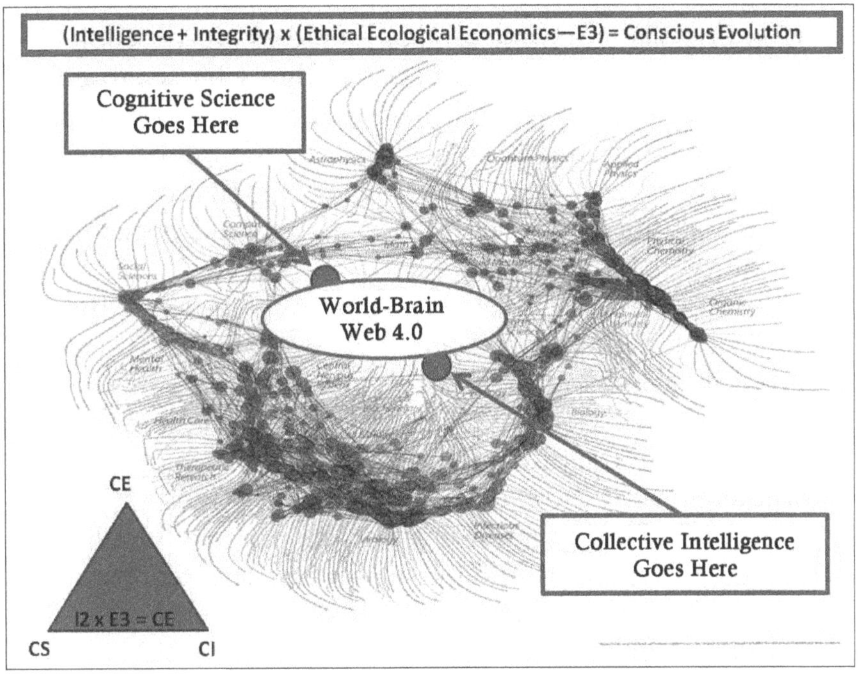

(Intelligence + Integrity) x (Ethical Ecological Economics—E3) = Conscious Evolution

Cognitive Science Goes Here

World-Brain Web 4.0

Collective Intelligence Goes Here

CE

$I2 \times E3 = CE$

CS   CI

Figure 3. Scattered Knowledge.

THE FUTURE OF HUMINT (BROADLY AND PROPERLY DEFINED)

HUMINT (broadly and properly defined) will be the heart, soul, and brain of 21st century intelligence, not only within governments, but within all eight tribes of intelligence. In addition to CI and Security, I explicitly include both analysts of individual techni-

9

cal collection disciplines and all-source analysts; and consumers at every level from President to action officer.[29]

HUMINT at the strategic level will be about smart nations, clever continents, and the world brain. At the operational level it will be about multinational information-sharing and sense-making to achieve mutual objectives by harmonizing up to $1 trillion a year in spending via an online Global Range of Needs Table that harmonizes organizational budgets by location and policy objective, while also inducing direct charitable giving by the 80 percent of the one billion rich who do not currently give. The harmonization will occur voluntarily through the use of shared decision support.[30]

At the tactical level, HUMINT will become the queen of the intelligence chessboard, providing direct support to the king—*any* decisionmaker—by harnessing the distributed intelligence of all humans in all languages all the time—both those in the specific area of interest, and those outside who have something to contribute—and by restoring human primacy in relation to all technical intelligence operations, technical intelligence will excel *with* HUMINT, not alone.

Financially and technically, HUMINT should control and redirect signal intelligence (SIGINT), imagery intelligence (IMINT), and measurements and signatures intelligence (MASINT) because for the first time, the managers of HUMINT will understand **the HUMINT Trifecta**:

1. Educate and nurture the all-source analysts *and* consumers;
2. Demand ROI metrics for all sources and methods of intelligence. This will cut technical funding in half to the benefit of education, HUMINT, and research; and

3. Provide the decisionmaker with concise, contextually-grounded all-source insights in a "just enough, just in time" manner that leaves no decision—whether of policy, acquisition, or operations—without a firm foundation[31] such that we eliminate fraud, waste, and abuse.

The future of HUMINT lies in creating the world brain[32] and the EarthGame™,[33] with clandestine and covert activities playing the vital but fractional role they merit in the larger context of all humans, all minds, all the time. *Without HUMINT, most technical intelligence is noise. Without HUMINT, decisions will continue to be made in a vacuum, at great cost.*

Figure 4 is the culmination of my 30 or so years in the intelligence business. I will not belabor the fact that many other nations are vastly superior to the United States in their management of "full spectrum HUMINT," but I will mention two: the People's Republic of China (PRC), and the Islamic Republic of Iran.[34] What I now understand is how very fragmented the single discipline of HUMINT has become. It has no leadership of the whole, in part because the OMB gave up the "M" in the 1980s, if not sooner, and in part because within the IC and the DoD, we are still organized into stovepipes that do not interact well among themselves.[35] This leaves the President—and all cabinet secretaries including the Secretary of Defense—without any decision support at all when it comes to the core presidential duty of ensuring that the USG is trained, equipped, and organized to preserve and protect the United States.[36] *Put most directly, managing HUMINT as I suggest will immediately enhance decisionmaking by the President, the cabinet secretaries the congressional committees, and field commanders.*

"Full Spectrum" Human Intelligence

Clandestine HUMINT
Covert Action HUMINT
Offensive Counterintelligence
Covert   Defensive Counterintelligence
"Hides"

HTT   DOCEX
                             Overt $ 50%
DefAtt   SME
ITT   LNO $ 50%

Open Source Intelligence (OSINT)
is Human Source, Not Technical

■ Citizen as Sensor
■ Soldier as Sensor (Overt/Open Signals)
■ Operational Test & Evaluation
■ Inspector-General (Org, USG, Int'l)
■ Security Observation/Remote Webcams
■ Document Exploitation/Imagery
■ Overt Subject-Matter Experts (SME)
■ Defense Attaches, MAG, Liaison, TDY
■ Human Terrain Teams (HTT)
■ Interrogator-Translator Teams (ITT)
■ Soldier as Sensor (Covert "Hides")
■ Defensive Counterintelligence
■ Offensive Counterintelligence
■ Covert Action HUMINT   U-2, N-2, J-2
■ Clandestine HUMINT   as the "Hub"

Education, Lessons Learned, Research, & Training are Foundation for Intelligence

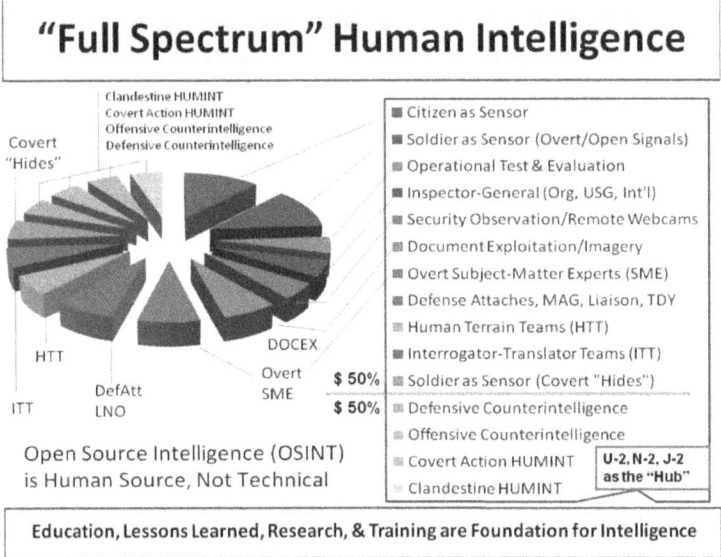

Note: LNO = Liaison Officer, SME = Subject Matter Expert.

Figure 4. Integrated Full-Spectrum HUMINT Management.[37]

As I discuss each of the 15 HUMINT elements, I am acutely conscious of the failure of our national educational system. I believe we have failed our children (and consequently our recruiting pool for the U.S. Army) in three ways: First, we have allowed local government insiders to cheat the educational system by providing tax breaks, public land and public services to corporations, reaping handsome commissions and fees for themselves, while dramatically reducing the tax base that supports locally-funded education.[38] Second, we have failed to update a school system initially designed around the needs of farmers (summers off) and then of factories (rote learning), and more or less beaten much of the creativity and curiosity out of our children by the time they enter the fifth grade.[39] They have to fight their way out of the box we built around them. We should be in year-round education, with apprenticeships that nurture whole-person growth with a full range of human trade and professional skills that are needed for localized resilience. We should be emphasizing team learning, project learning, challenge examinations based on distance learning, and real-world problem-solving. We should be teaching the art of global multinational information access. Third, we have broken the links between the natural world — the Earth, the human world termed by some as the *anthroposphere*[40] — and the world of faith, spirit and mind, be it an agnostic *noosphere*[41] or a form of religion.[42]

Our children, in brief, have been raised in a bubble, and have not learned how to do whole systems thinking in a spontaneous or collective fashion. At the same time, we have broken the accountability and transparency links between those who pay taxes, and the government officials that spend that revenue.

In my view, the future of HUMINT demands that we create an Open Source Agency (OSA) as called for by the 9/11 Commission,[43] and that we make OSINT our top priority for both funding and the attention of our national and defense intelligence leaders, as called for by the Aspin-Brown Commission.[44] It is only in the context of what OSINT can do, that clandestine HUMINT and the other slices of HUMINT can be fully effective. As provided for in the Smart Nation-Safe Nation Act,[45] an OSA funded by the DoD would provide the following HUMINT foundation for all eight tribes:

1. Office of Information Sharing Treaties and Agreements (OISTA);[46]
2. Office of the Assistant Secretary General for Decision Support (ASG DS) within the United Nations (UN), and a UN-validated Global

Range of Needs Table to harmonize U.S. $1 trillion a year in spending by others;[47]

3. Multinational Decision Support Center (MDSC), along with regional centers (one per continent);[48]

4. A Multinational Decision Support University (MDSU) to train executives (at all levels) from all nations and all eight tribes of intelligence, *together*.[49]

I will begin my review of the 15 slices of HUMINT in the 21st century with a quotation from Senator Daniel Patrick Moynihan (D-NY), who invited me to testify[50] to the Moynihan Commission.[51] From their letter of transmittal:

> The Commission's report is unanimous. It contains recommendations for actions by the Executive Branch and the Legislative Branch, with the object of protecting and reducing secrecy in an era when open sources make a plenitude of information available as never before in history. [52]

The United States has lost the ability to intelligently collect, process, exploit, and analyze global knowledge, all of it originating with indigenous humans speaking 34 core languages[53] and thousands of additional dialects and micro-languages. This has happened because the political leadership of both parties has been captured by Wall Street and the military-industrial complex to the detriment of diplomacy, development, and democracy, all three of which demand rigorous respect for all relevant information (96 percent of which is openly available according to General Anthony Zinni, USMC [Ret.]). His hard-earned and practical observation is vital to the future of HUMINT:

80 percent of what I needed to know as CINCENT [Commander in Chief, U.S. Central Command] I got from open sources rather than classified reporting. And within the remaining 20 percent, if I knew what to look for,[54] I found another 16 percent. At the end of it all, classified intelligence provided me, at best, with 4 percent of my command knowledge. [55]

HUMINT, since World War II has been misdirected. Separately, I have published an early evaluation of why OSINT is so important to every aspect of military policy, acquisition, and operations, and will not belabor the point here other than to state my view that radical force structure redesign is not properly supported by military or civilian intelligence today, because its practitioners do not know how to train, equip, and organize in order to provide whole of government decision support, or how to serve every level of decision across every mission area, both military and civilian.[56] *The time has come to redefine HUMINT concepts, doctrine, and practices.*

HUMINT: DEFINING AND MANAGING THE FIFTEEN SLICES

Today each of the 15 slices is being managed in isolation, and that must not be allowed to continue. The DoD can fix this for a whole of government benefit.

Citizen as Sensor and Sense-Maker.

In 1986, while I was managing Project GEORGE (Smiley) in the Office of Information Technology (OIT) at the CIA, I defined the needs for information technology (IT) support to both clandestine opera-

15

tions and all-source analysis, and that is where I had my blinding flash of insight on the challenges of data entry. The bottom line is that no one government, and less so any one agency, can afford, understand, or execute global data entry. The only possible solution is one that harnesses the distributed intelligence of the whole earth, i.e., all humans, all minds.[57]

In 1994, I realized that it is not possible to have smart spies in the context of a dumb nation, and in 2006, working with Congressman Rob Simmons (R-CT), I realized that 50 percent of the dots which need to be connected to prevent the next September 11, 2001 (9/11), or to respond to a natural disaster such as Katrina, will be bottom-up dots from citizens and police on the beat. Those dots have no place to go today in 2010, 9 years after 9/11. We need *unclassified* state-based fusion centers in which sensitive information from all eight tribes can be processed,[58] and that is why the Smart Nation-Safe Nation Act[59] that I devised includes $1.5 Billion to create 50 state-based Citizen Intelligence Centers and Networks to be manned by the National Guard (which can hold both local law enforcement commissions and foreign intelligence clearances), and another $1.5 Billion funding for foreign open source information acquisition and processing initiatives that harness all that the UN system and our multinational partners can help us access, exploit, and share from schoolhouse to White House, and worldwide.

The one thing the United States can do for our future generations is to get a grip on HUMINT in all its forms, and help the eight demographic challengers[60] to implement the world brain and the Earth Game™ via free cell phones for the poor, and call centers that teach the poor "one cell call at a time."[61]

A LINUX quote can be adapted here. They say

"Put enough eyeballs on it, and no bug is invisible." [62] I say, Put enough minds to work, and no threat, no policy, no challenge will withstand the collective intelligence of We.

From a HUMINT perspective, there are at least three priceless (hence, unaffordable by any one government) citizen-based contributions to national intelligence: as a source of personnel; as a source of overt observation; and as a source of clandestine and counterintelligence help. The USG has failed over time to be effective across all three of these vital domains.[63] This is one reason I believe in universal service (and the right to bear arms) as the foundation for liberty within a republic with a sovereign people.[64]

The near-term importance of the citizen-observer is not well-understood by leaders in government or corporations or even most nonprofit organizations in part because those leaders are 10-20 years behind in their understanding of what modern technology makes possible. In brief, the spread of cellular telephones, including cell towers in remote regions powered by solar energy[65] or ambient energy,[66] has made possible the integration of three wildly productive factors: citizen "eyes on," web data templates, and cellular short message service (SMS) inputs with geospatial attributes and photographs.

Figure 5 shows a very short list of applications that exist today, many of them award-winning and all of them suitable for rapid migration to all locations and across all issues.[67] Educating the rest of the world, free, is part of this slice.[68]

Blood Testing	Mobile phone hacked to be a portable blood tester capable of detecting HIV, malaria, other illnesses
Child Malnutrition	UNICEF, Net Squared (USAID 1st Prize)
City Problems	ClickFix transparency anywhere in the world
Corrupt Officials	Indonesia pilot project.
Crisis Response	InSTEAD GeoChat
Crop Disease	Africa pilot, treating disease via cell phone
Disease	12 sources, close to 100 diseases, each plotted individually, can zoom in on any country
Election Irregularities	VoterReport India, Electoral Commission Intervention, Forged Votes, Inflammatory Speech, Other Irregularities, Violence, Voter Bribing, Voter Name Missing, Voting Machine Problems
Environmental Monitoring	Mobile phone photos plus GPS enhance citizen-scientist responsiveness, utility, and credibility
Flood Warning	FloodSMS
Genocide	Eight stages start with easy to detect demonization
Roadway Fatalities	SafeRoadMaps
Sexual Harassment	Egypt pilot project
Traffic	Many locations, volume, noise, pollution
Vandalism	Anonymous texting as it happens, England
Violence	India, elsewhere, on verge of 911 SMS plotting
War Actions in Gaza	Aljazeera, distinguishes among Air Strikes, Announcement, Deaths, Israeli Casualties, Israeli Forces, IAid, Casualties, Protests, Rocket Attacks.

Figure 5. Direct Cell Phone Report Systems Using SMS.

Soldier as Sensor (Overt/Open Signals).

In this monograph, the term "Soldier" embraces both military and civilian personnel serving domestically or overseas. The concept of the "strategic corporal" is well-established,[69] both by Field Marshall Erwin Rommel, and more recently (1999) by General Charles Krulak, USMC.[70] The concept of "commander's intent" is also well-established, having been given global recognition by General Gray.[71]

However, our Soldiers continue to be treated as a quantity good rather than a quality being. Up to this point, we have trained, equipped, and organized our military around high-cost, high-maintenance technologies without regard to the needs or abilities of the individual Soldier, and we have not treated the individual Soldier with the respect each merits when properly educated, trained, led, *and listened to*. The Soldier is the ultimate HUMINT asset.[72]

Especially troubling to me is the continuing resistance to the concept developed by the Swedish military and enhanced by myself: Multinational, Multiagency, Multidisciplinary, Multidomain Information-Sharing and Sense-Making (M4IS2).[73]

In my view, whole of government training, equipping, and organizing, led by the U.S. military and using U.S. military training facilities, can most fruitfully be enhanced by making it multinational and multifunctional in nature. A stellar example of success is offered by the annual Strong Angel exercise, an annual series of civil-military demonstrations that show methods for civilian and military agencies around the world to work effectively together within a disaster response. It is especially noteworthy for providing TOOZL, an analytic and communications toolkit on a flash-drive, consisting of Free/Open Source Software (F/OSS) that anyone can use without cost.[74]

Here again, we see the vital need for education and training in the context of a national strategy, a military strategy, a robust nationwide education system, continuing adult education, and multinational information-sharing.

HUMINT starts in the classroom and is then augmented in real-life. It is essential to the success of the secret elements of HUMINT that we plan for the fullest possible exploitation of the nonsecret elements. Patrolling by infantry is how we create a 360-degree *human* safety network.[75] Unfortunately, we have allowed our force reconnaissance—our deep humans—to be reduced in numbers, experience, and utility. On the battlefield, it is *force reconnaissance* that emplaces "close in" technical devices.

Operational Test & Evaluation (OT&E).

I realize that operational test and evaluation (OT&E) must fall under the oversight of the Undersecretary of Defense for Intelligence [USD(I)] because speaking truth to power cannot apply only to "red" forces, or to "white," "yellow," and "green" forces, but to our own "blue" forces as well. Lies kill one's comrades. We must stop lying to ourselves!

This first became apparent to me in 1988 when the MCIA pioneered strategic generalizations about the real-world: bridge-loading limits (30-ton limits on average across the Third World); line-of-sight averages (under 1,000 meters); hot and humid aviation days (the DoD standard for OT&E is warm and not humid)—the list is long.

What the four Services build and buy in isolation

from one another has virtually nothing to do with the actual 10 high-level threats to humanity, not even to the single interstate conflict threat (number four on that now universally-applauded list). Indeed, the Services have been caught manipulating threat databases so as to justify bigger systems with more complex elements, to the point that the systems cannot go over any normal bridge in the Third World; need one contractor per Soldier to maintain in the field; and are irrelevant against 80 percent of actual needs. This is unprofessional.

Despite the best efforts of the Joint Forces Command (JFCOM) and of course the Undersecretary of Defense for Acquisition [USD(A)], the DoD is easily 20 years away from being globally-relevant and effective at operations other than war (OOTW), now more fashionably called stabilization and reconstruction (S&R) operations, with a side dish of irregular warfare (IRWF), not to be confused with information operations, (IO—a mutant mix of public relations and psychological operations on steroids, with zero intelligence).

I finally realized the insanity of a multiservice array of capabilities that are not understood by Presidents or even the commanders who oversee them when I learned that we sent 10 tomahawks to kill Osama bin Laden. They took 6 hours to reach his camp, passing over Pakistan, which assuredly alerted him. More recently, we have been using drones to kill clusters of individuals, mostly bystanders. We are oblivious to the long-term human impact of our actions.

I have come to the conclusion that not only must all weapons, mobility, and communications systems be validated by the USD(I) across the requirements and procurements process and in OT&E, but that specific operational plans require USD(I) validation as well. We have to stop carpet bombing villages, and get down to one man - one bullet efficacy while nurturing everyone else.

Inspector-General (Organizational, USG, International).

Inspector-General (IG) endeavors in the past have spanned the full spectrum from over-zealous investigations of minor infractions through largely ceremonial and entirely predictable inspections of administrative minutia. More recently, efforts by the Director of National Intelligence (DNI) to integrate IG functions across the 16 agencies nominally under his authority, and the equally recent emergence of interest in transnational or regional IG collaboration within select intelligence, military, and law enforcement communities, are both worthy of note.[76]

Every graduate degree in public administration requires a course in program evaluation, and it is there, not in regulatory compliance and after-the-fact investigation, that the IG can make a real contribution. The IG, like each of the other slices in the larger HUMINT pie, must be an integrated part of the totality of full-spectrum HUMINT with an intimate constructive—not punitive—relationship with and among all slices.

A director of the OMB—which has done some good things in its search for common solutions—might consider the varied IG cadres as an extension of OMB's reach, and work hard to restore the management function of OMB while also redirecting the IG function toward improved remediation and oversight of requirements definition, capabilities acquisition, and operational efficacy.

The GAO can no longer be shut out of the USIC. Easily 80 percent of secrecy is being used to avoid accountability,[77] and as paradoxical as it may sound, transparency is something that is desperately needed within the secret world, at least with respect to financial inputs and consequential outputs. In my view, at least half, if not two-thirds, of the entire USIC budget could be, and should be, available for redirection by the President toward education, whole of government and multinational intelligence (decision support) that is not secret, and research focused on the eradication of the 10 high-level threats to humanity, eight of which are now ignored.

At the same time, we need to question the entirety of our military assistance budget. In brief, we need an IG inspection of our fundamental assumptions about war and peace in the 21st century.

At the strategic level, the IGs should all be in alliance with the GAO, OMB, and General Services Administration (GSA), seeking to define completely new 21st century objectives that are transformative of the means, ways, and ends of government, not just seeking to be more efficient and legal with old means, old ways, and old ends.

Security Observation/Remote Webcams/ Floating Periscopes.

Humans are the essential element in security observation and in the exploitation of distributed security cameras including the new wireless (some solar-powered) webcams. Based on my own experience, I find three general areas that could be improved: First, no one country can be covered by a single security plan, even one that distinguishes among mission, facilities, movement, and individuals. In one particular country, we found the need for three separate security surveillance and preparation plans, one for the north, one for the south, and one for the capital city. Indeed, I am reminded of General Zinni's extremely useful observation that Vietnam was actually six wars: (1) Swamp War, (2) Paddy War, (3) Jungle War, (4) Plains War, (5) Saigon War, and (6) DMZ War; each with its own lessons, tactics, and sometimes equipment differences.[78]

Second, we have been slow to empower our distributed forces with both modern security surveillance technology, and the *tactical* processing power needed to do "face trace" or find other anomalies that might be missed by the human eye.[79] In contrast, the Metropolitan Police of London (Scotland Yard) have dramatically reduced crime and increased arrests by using a city-wide array of surveillance cameras with very clever humans exploiting them from a central location that also has access to distributed culturally-astute interpreters of body language in context.

Third, between solar power, relay stations, and satellite communications, there is no reason why we cannot field persistent ground surveillance, for example, along the Somali coast. In my view, we are spending too much time worrying about close-in force protection, and not nearly enough time thinking about and practicing distributed observation for early warning. I might mention in this regard that when I was asked to review the new counterterrorism plan for one Service in the aftermath of 9/11, I found the Service planners to have doubled-up everything that existed previously, with zero innovation. My short response was move your *virtual* perimeter out 100 klicks, brief every waitress and gas station attendant and truck driver in that circle that you can, and give them a number that is answered 24/7, as well as an incentive to call in.

Security is a form of static HUMINT combined with on demand HUMINT, and only a robust educational program can make it effective.[80] Working with elements of the UN Department of Safety and Security (DSS), I have found a real hunger for creating completely new forms of smart security that emphasize the human factor rather than the physical. We can all do better.

Document Exploitation/Imagery.

Based on conversations I have had with peacekeepers and others, we appear to have enormous opportunities for improvement. I am told, for example, that it still takes 4-6 weeks for 10 pages of captured Dari documents to be translated and returned to the tactical commander, there being no practical or responsive Dari translation capability within Afghanistan.[81]

I have two reactions: First, given the number of individuals living in Afghanistan that speak and read Dari while also being reasonably fluent with English, I see our security mind-sets interfering with tactical needs for rapid exploitation of captured documents. There are a number of ways to achieve time and risk-based security while meeting the needs of the tactical commanders. I can do Dari translations from the field within 4-6 hours. Why is this still a problem? Old minds and processes.

My second reaction is to wonder why we have not implemented a global grid using *www.telelanguage. com*, and field digitization (to include pen-based digitization) that can go directly from the field to a Dari translator on call in that given instant. Figure 6 shows an illustration of generic capabilities since 1997.

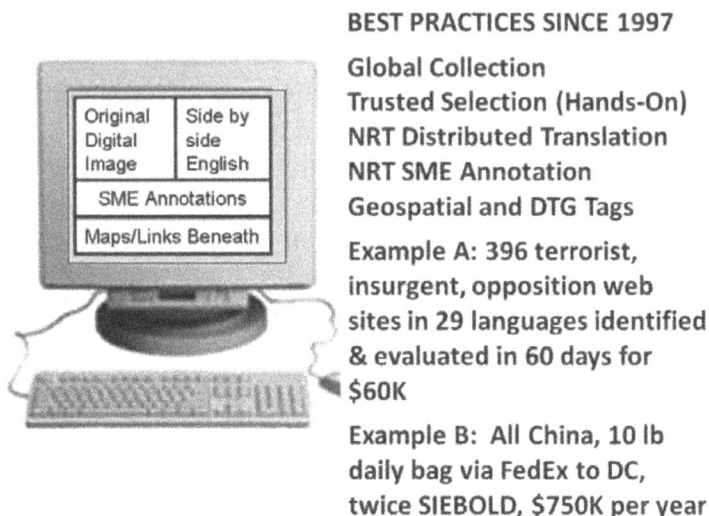

Original Digital Image	Side by side English
SME Annotations	
Maps/Links Beneath	

BEST PRACTICES SINCE 1997

Global Collection

Trusted Selection (Hands-On)

NRT Distributed Translation

NRT SME Annotation

Geospatial and DTG Tags

Example A: 396 terrorist, insurgent, opposition web sites in 29 languages identified & evaluated in 60 days for $60K

Example B: All China, 10 lb daily bag via FedEx to DC, twice SIEBOLD, $750K per year

Figure 6. Global Collection, Translation, and Annotation.[82]

This area is urgently in need of a multinational burden-sharing network. The current 11-nation capability is trivial—90 nations is my standard.[83]

All-Source Analysts & Global Experts.

Although the classical definition of HUMINT emphasizes clandestine collection and covert action (agents of influence, propaganda, paramilitary operations), I believe that in an age when 80-90 percent of the information from humans is overt, and secret intelligence provides, at best, 4 percent of a combatant commander's information, we have to rethink HUMINT.

I submit that both the CIA and the DoD are in error

in their current approach to manning. The CIA tends to hire very young people unproven at clandestine or analytic tradecraft, while the DoD uses enlisted personnel for many tasks that in my view require a liberal arts college education.

I believe that over the next 10 years we must migrate away from putting new hires into anything other than OSINT exploitation, and emphasize mid-career hires for the senior all-source analytic positions, as well as HUMINT collection and CI positions (the latter retaining their life's pattern as legitimate cover).

At the same time, we must empower all-source analysts with the resources and the multinational social skills with which to leverage global experts regardless of nationality, and with the ability to draw on the MDSC for reach-back to all eight tribes of any given country.

As a general rule of thumb, I believe each division manager should have $1 million a year; that each branch manager should have $250,000 a year; and that each individual analyst, no matter how junior, should have $50,000 to spend, on a mix of external expertise, combined with travel to conferences or in-house seminars and sounding boards—anything that is legal to buy.[84]

It costs less than $1,000 to identify the top 100 published experts in any field based on citation of their work, and another $1,000 or so to communicate with each of the published experts so as to identify the top 25-100 unpublished experts. Every analyst should have such a network on call.

In the overt arena, clandestine case officers skilled at tradecraft cannot cut it. It takes a substantive expert with tangible rewards to offer in the form of legally shareable information, privileged access, unconventional insights, or straight-up modest consulting fees (as little as $250 or as much as $5,000) to work the global overt expertise grid.

Notably absent from my thinking are defense contractors and their costs.[85] I am skeptical about the value of people sitting in offices, and I am also a strong proponent of centralized OSINT contract management along with rigorous metrics for accountability, as well as a "buy once for all" OSINT acquisition system. I believe the U.S. Army must develop both strategists and foreign area specialists within its own ranks, not as an out-sourced function, and must nurture these individuals over the course of a career, not "one tour and out."

Defense Attaches, Technical Liaison.

This category includes every human assigned any form of international or interagency responsibility, and I especially wish to include our officers assigned to military groups (MILGRP), to the schools of other nations, and to all external billets including fellowships at think tanks, command exchange tours, and so on. Civilian intelligence personnel distributed among the combatant commands are now under the Director of the DIA oversight, and that is a good start for the DoD. Country teams remain a kludge of single representatives from multiple agencies that often out-number (and out-spend) the diplomats, and by no stretch of the imagination can any embassy be considered to be coherent in how every person is harmonized to create a whole.[86]

In my view, we are long overdue for a top to bottom review of how the DoD as a whole, and each individual Service, handle the selection, assignment, and on-going oversight and exploitation of all officers as well as noncommissioned and enlisted personnel serving in external billets. The same is true for all the other agencies, most of which are incapable of addressing contingencies or fielding task forces that are trained, equipped, and organized for short- to long-term operations under conditions more often than not hazardous.[87]

For this group, very possibly the "center of gravity" for HUMINT as a whole, I have a few thoughts:

1. There is no substitute for continuity in-country and on the desk in Washington, DC. We need to get serious about deep language training and repetitive area tours. Ideally embassy personnel should have 6-8 year assignments with assured promotions, and staggered tours so the second officer arrives midway through the tour of the person being replaced.

2. MILGRPs are a wasted asset from an IO point of view. I had an excellent talk with a MILGRP liaison officer at the U.S. Pacific Command (USPACOM) in 1994, and learned that MILGRPs have no information sharing or sense-making responsibilities to speak of — they are there to focus on moving U.S. military equipment into the local pipeline. That needs to change.

3. Even if the rest of the USIC and the rest of the USG are not ready for whole of government operations, the DoD needs to take the lead. A good start would be to create a special sense-making unit within the DIA/DH that deals overtly and respectfully with every single DoD body (and in the ideal, with every other USG body assigned to an external billet worldwide), while treating the 137 Defense Attaché locations as the core mass, building from there.

Human Terrain Teams.

Rarely does one encounter a program that is at once so well-intentioned and also so very badly managed as the Human Terrain Teams (HTT) program. While there must certainly be two sides to the story, and a good manager will engage in compassionate listening and a 360 degree evaluation before making changes, I understand from multiple sources that this program is out-of-control to the point of being dangerous to both the individuals being misdirected into the program, and the commanders and troops ostensibly receiving this support. I believe this program must immediately be subordinated to the Director of the DIA and therein subordinated to the DIA/DH, which should be expanded to provide leadership and management, including resource oversight, for all 15 slices of HUMINT. In its own words,

> [Human Terrain System] HTS is a new proof-of-concept program, run by the U.S. Army Training and Doctrine Command (TRADOC), and serving the joint community. The near-term focus of the HTS program is to improve the military's ability to understand the highly complex local socio-cultural environment in the areas where they are deployed; however, in the long-term, HTS hopes to assist the U.S. government in understanding foreign countries and regions prior to an engagement within that region.[88]

TRADOC is running this as an experimental program, and they do not appear to have the knowledge — or even the network to acquire the knowledge — needed to manage this potentially valuable global grid of culturally-astute SMEs.[89]

I am troubled by the various photographs that contrast heavily-armed, heavily-armored individuals wearing sunglasses and trying to do the "hearts and minds" deal without the skills to assimilate themselves and be effective. Overall, program management, personnel selection, insistence on clearances, a marginal training program, and very badly managed in-country assignments and oversight appear to demand an urgent and complete redirection of HTT. The existing web pages are replete with known errors,[90] inflated claims, and a reading list that would make any real anthropologist weep.[91] This program appears to need a complete makeover.[92] *Done right, HTT should be inter-disciplinary and multinational, and should not require clearances at all.*

Interrogator-Translator Teams.

I have a special affection for interrogator-translator teams (ITT), and a real sense of awe at the capabilities of new forms of forward-deployed tactical analysts who, among other achievements, sniffed out Saddam Hussein's final hide-out, something no national intelligence capability was able to do.

For the purposes of this monograph, I want to broaden the ITT category to include military police (MP), civil affairs (CA), combat engineers (CE), and all that come into contact with both prisoners of war (POW)—which in the Marine Corps is an S-1/Adjutant housekeeping job rather than an S-2 intelligence exploitation job—and with civilians, including our logisticians (who are constantly starved for intelligence support at the same time that they have so much to offer in terms of practical insights about access and trafficability).

In peacetime, it has often troubled me that ITT as well as CI personnel tend to be farmed out to take care of all the temporary additional duty (TAD) demands in a given headquarters, and at the battalion level to find the least-desired Marine officers going into the S-2 job. Of course my knowledge is dated, but some things never change.

I believe the time has come to both fence all intelligence personnel from nonintelligence assignments, and to dramatically augment the assignment of intelligence personnel down to the squad, platoon, and company level. I have been enormously impressed by the initiative of some company commanders in Afghanistan, taking everyone with an IQ above 120 (or whatever number needed) to get at least six smarter-than-average individuals, to create company level ad hoc field intelligence analysis units.[93]

I participated in two force structure studies when serving the Marine Corps as the second-ranking civilian in Marine Corps intelligence, and my arguments for reducing shooters and increasing thinkers consistently went nowhere. Now is the time for the USD(I) and the D/DIA to take a fresh look at HUMINT across the board, taking great care to define HUMINT as all humans, all minds, all the time, and working from there. HUMINT is no longer something that can be isolated as an arcane specialization. Not only can the commander not delegate intelligence,[94] but the intelligence staff officer must conceive and execute a new form of HUMINT campaign plan that simultaneously educates, trains, informs, empowers, and ultimately protects every member of the interagency team that is being supported, and that is both conscious of—and able to exploit—every human several times removed in their respective networks.[95]

Soldier as Sensor (Patrolling, Force Reconnaissance, Covert "Hides").

Patrolling is a fundamental element of infantry operations, and appears to rise and fall in cycles. Its companion, force reconnaissance, also tends to rise and fall. There is no substitute for a human brain attached to human eyes and ears, particularly when real-time contextual understanding and warning is needed. While unmanned aerial vehicles (UAVs) and forward air controllers (FAC) and aerial observers (AO) can be most helpful, it is the human on the ground that produces "ground truth," a "360 degree" appreciation that cannot be achieved by any combination of technologies, close-in or remote. This is as true of peacekeeping operations as it is of full-spectrum hostilities.[96]

Professor Richard Aldrich, whose chapter, "From Ireland to Bosnia: Intelligence Support for UK Low Intensity Operations," has a special lesson for us with respect to the importance of placing soldiers in covert "hides."

> In both Ireland and Bosnia, units on the ground appreciated the importance of a holistic approach to intelligence. Intelligence was vital to support even the smallest units and every patrol devoted time and attention to intelligence gathering. Patrols were often high-profile affairs whose main function initially was to reassure the public and to assert authority. In both environments, patrols required intelligence support from covert observation points to reinforce their security. Substantial numbers of covert observation posts had to be established in order to reduce the number of patrol incidents. In Ireland, soldiers, often trained by the members of the SAS, would lie in cover with binoculars, high-powered telescopes, and night vision devices for days or weeks

on end in order to observe specific individuals or areas. Such covert observation posts could link with patrols in order to dominate an area. But the work exposed them to attack if their location was uncovered by passing civilians.[97]

He goes on to observe:

In both Ireland and Bosnia, tactical intelligence gathering was lent an additional importance because the flow of intelligence from the higher echelons to those on the ground was weak. Intelligence at ground level flowed up, but not down.[98]

I also believe that a great deal more can be done in using force reconnaissance to emplace close-in remote monitors, including webcams and live audio devices, in enemy encampments and criminal enclaves.[99]

Defensive Counterintelligence.

We now cross the line from the first 11 overt elements of HUMINT, and move into the final four, each replete with classified sources and methods that cannot be discussed here.[100]

My first point is that CI is a completely distinct specialization, not to be confused with clandestine HUMINT. The first requires the detection, *without warning*, of the in-house suspect of illegal or even unsanctioned activities and disclosures potentially threatening to the United States.[101]

Despite the fact that Presidents (e.g., Ronald Reagan)[102] and Senators (e.g., Durbin, Hatch, Rockefeller, and Shelby)[103] leak and destroy sensitive capabilities overnight and without any recrimination, defensive CI is supposed to be the pro-active means by which we prevent, detect, and deceive those who seek to betray our national security enterprise from within. Contractors, in my view, are 80 percent of the challenge.

Aldrich Ames (CIA) and Robert Hansen (Federal Bureau of Investigation [FBI]) are noteworthy failures of defensive CI. Ames was driving a Jaguar and paid cash for a $450,000 house. When asked to investigate his claim that his Colombian wife inherited the money, the CIA Chief of Station (COS) in Bogota blew off the request. Hansen, a study in contradictions, from ostensibly devout Catholic to worshipping a stripper, failed to arouse any serious attention.

Defensive counterintelligence, as best I can tell, has three major failings today. First, it is considered — at least within the CIA — to be a backwater and a dumping ground, an undesirable assignment, and one that I believe still lacks good leadership, not for lack of good people, but for lack of appreciation. Second, the culture of the U.S. intelligence community is one of "once in, can do no wrong."[104] This is compounded by a lack of contractor-focused CI.[105] Third, the data access system of systems of the U.S. intelligence community is not designed to track individual access or specific document access across the board. Individuals receive generic "CODEWORD" clearances and then have relative carte blanche access. We are not using information technology well for CI, either defense *or* offensive.

To appreciate defensive CI and needed reforms, read *Merchants of Treason: America's Secrets for Sale,*[106] and *Traitors Among Us: Inside the Spycatcher's World.*[107] There are other books, but these two capture the essence of why defensive counterintelligence really matters.

Defensive CI is much easier if we reduce unnecessary secrecy.

Offensive Counterintelligence.

Offensive CI is very similar to clandestine HU-MINT, but with a very special focus that is rarely taken seriously. It demands the obsessive identification of individuals responsible for penetrating our own organizations, rather than—as with defensive counterintelligence—the identification of our own nationals who might be vulnerable to recruitment for the purpose of betraying secrets, whether wittingly or unwittingly.[108]

Within the CIA, this can be a dumping ground, but more often than not it is simply an additional duty and not given the emphasis that it merits. In my own case, it was one of two full-time jobs to which I was, assigned and I was literally the only person in the CIA paid to think about penetrating the U.S. targeting element within the clandestine service of a specific denied area country.

An emerging aspect of offensive, as well as defensive, CI is to be found in the cyberwar and electronic security arena. The Chinese appear to have mastered the art of riding the electrical grid into computers that are otherwise not on the Internet. Based on my own experience with the Special Communications Center (SPINTCOM) at the MCIA, it is all too easy to feed naïve lance corporals free games that they then insert into the SPINTCOM computers to fritter away the late night hours. The complexity of the cyberwar arena is not well-understood in the United States. I tried to flag this with a $1 billion a year budget in 1995, pulling together expert advice from, among others, the top NSA consultant on cyber security. [109] Today, the NSA is asking for $12 billion a year, and in all likelihood will focus more on expanding its access to every datum about every person in America, and be less successful at helping to create a fireproof national grid. The situation is not made any better by the fact that virtually all of our supervisory control and data acquisition (SCADA) systems are on the open Internet as a result of companies deciding in the 1980s and 1990s that they could save money by not having stand-alone systems impervious to hacking, doing so in part because we lack a national industrial security strategy and policy.

My personal inclination is to place security and defensive CI under one deputy director, while placing offensive CI, covert action, and clandestine HUMINT under another deputy director. The third—and the principal deputy director— would manage the first 11 slices of overt HUMINT. I believe that managing overt HUMINT together with CI and clandestine HUMINT will add enormous value at virtually no additional cost.[110]

Covert Action HUMINT.

There is no finer overview on covert action that is legally available to the public than that of Alfred Cumming.[111] Traditionally, since the National Security Act of 1947, covert action has been (in theory) the exclusive province of the CIA and defined in general terms as agents of influence (pushing governments to do things against their own best interests but favored by U.S. policymakers); propaganda (media manipulation); and paramilitary operations including coups, instability operations, and sabotage of perceived threats (e.g., a nuclear or bio-chemical facility). Support activities such as Air America or Southern Air Transport, and administrative activities such as money laundering (to include the creation or complete subordination of entire banks), the acquisition of enemy weapons for use by our own "false flag" forces, and more recently, rendition and torture, all fall in this arena.

I am persuaded by my own direct experience and a lifetime of reading, that U.S. policymakers are neither sufficiently informed nor ethically grounded, and therefore should not be authorizing covert actions, with two exceptions: the capture or assassination of key terrorist or gang leaders, and the interdiction of key ingredients of chemical, biological, radiological, and nuclear (CBRN) weapons of mass destruction (WMD).[112]

Covert actions violate the Geneva Convention, and harken back to the first era of national intelligence, war by other means. The very definition of covert action, "an activity or activities of the United States Government to influence political, economic, or military conditions abroad, where it is intended that the role of the United States Government will not be apparent or acknowledged publicity,"[113] is sufficient to suggest that covert action flies in the face of reality and sustainable consensus, and is largely unachievable—the USG cannot keep most secrets.

I include in covert action the funding of foreigners including foreign intelligence services that skim half the money and do evil in our name.[114] There is no substitute for reading Cumming's brilliant 9-page unclassified information paper.[115] The USG at this time lacks a strategic analytic model for understanding all 10 high-level threats to humanity and for harmonizing whole of government operations across all 12 core policies, and the USG is *largely* incapable of competently directing or executing covert actions, a few isolated operations notwithstanding.

Clandestine HUMINT.

From where I sit, the CIA has become useless. It refuses to abandon official cover, and it has proven incapable of scaling up nonofficial cover despite spending tens of millions of dollars, if not more, on up to 21 "pseudo-companies," 20 of which had to be shut down recently.[116] At the same time, the CIA's young case officers (C/O) and analysts deprive the CIA of any claim to special competence in HUMINT or all-source intelligence.[117] (The majority of the CIA analytic population now has less than 5 years employment at the CIA).

The DoD has until recently been unwilling to challenge the CIA, and kept most of its clandestine activities in a "hip-pocket" mode, as best I can tell from open sources. I believe that the DoD recognizes that if it wants to achieve world-class intelligence capabilities across the board, it must create them for itself; I write this monograph in part to help the DoD get it right.

In clandestine HUMINT, something I care deeply about, one needs to nurture leaders with open minds, and ideally leaders with very strong backgrounds in unconventional and irregular operations. Nothing handicaps clandestine HUMINT more than conventional mind-sets (i.e., uniformed leaders lacking clandestine experience), combined with lawyers afraid of their own shadows.[118]

I helped think about the clandestine service of the future, and saw clever recommendations ignored by a succession of CIA leaders. I recommend the creation of five slices of clandestine HUMINT, completely apart from the CIA, which I would convert into a single Classified Technical Intelligence Agency (CTIA), with one floor for each of the technical disciplines. The existing D/CIA could become the Deputy Director of National Intelligence (DDNI) for Technical Collection Management, while the D/DIA becomes the DDNI for Human and Open Source Collection Management, as well as All-Source Analysis.[119] My five recommended slices are:

- 1/5: Exceptionally talented entry-level citizens to serve indefinitely,
- 1/5: Mid-career U.S. citizens who have created their cover and access,
- 1/5: Mid-career foreign nationals who have created cover and access,
- 1/5: Mid-career case officers from other countries on rotation,
- 1/5: "It's just business;" one time business deals with no further ado.

Although CIA counterterrorism managers have done some very good hiring—I love the quote, "The college degree can come later," when hiring a foreigner with skills as a GS-15—on balance we need a new nonofficial service.[120]

HUMINT REQUIREMENTS AND COLLECTION MANAGEMENT

The USIC still does not have a serious requirements and collection management system (RCMS), not least because it considers the President its only "real" client; it has not trained a cadre of specialist requirements officers; and it persists is disregarding the value of OSINT while focusing on triage among the classified disciplines.

As a consultant to the IC map (ICMAP),[121] I pointed out the obvious, to little effect: that the IC was asking Question #4 of the following four questions, and ignoring the first three:
1. Can we FIND our answer in what we already have?
2. Can we GET our answer from someone we know?
3. Can we BUY our answer from the private sector?
4. WHICH classified systems should we TASK?

One of the unique advantages of HUMINT is its ability to receive and act on questions that are full of nuance, ambiguity, and complexity. Whereas the technical collection disciplines have to be told "what, when, and where," in the case of HUMINT, we only have to get three things right:
1. Understand the question,
2. Know who knows (the human source will sort out the nuances),
3. Connect the source with the client or debrief the source.

The major obstacles to HUMINT success are, in this order, our consumers, out-dated security guidelines, and ignorant lawyers.[122] To be successful, HUMINT managers must first educate all those "inside the wire."

HUMINT costs less, requires less time, and is much more responsive than technical collection, in part because with HUMINT, processing is embedded all along the human chain, from source to collector to analyst to consumer.

I will end this brief overview with the very last sentence of Jim Bamford's most recent book, *Body of*

Secrets: Anatomy of the Ultra-Secret National Security Agency:

> Eventually NSA may secretly achieve the ultimate in quickness, compatibility, and efficiency—a computer with petaflop and higher speeds shrunk into a container about a liter in size, and powered by only about ten watts of power: the human brain. [123]

HUMINT INTERDISCIPLINARY SUPPORT

Without getting into classified sources and methods, it is nonetheless necessary to emphasize the vital role that HUMINT plays in tipping off and supporting the technical collection disciplines. By way of context, the technical collection disciplines are vacuum cleaners in contrast to the precision of HUMINT, and suffer further from lacking the processing power to detect—in real-time—the anomalies and patterns or to translate—in real-time—the most important conversations. Hence, HUMINT can be—but usually is not—a vital force multiplier for the technical disciplines.

SIGINT relies heavily on HUMINT for the acquisition of code books from the field. It should rely heavily on HUMINT for the identification of specific communications devices that are being used to communicate using clandestine methods such as steganography, or bland conversation that is heavily laden with covert meaning; but in reality the HUMINT discipline has failed to develop as broadly and deeply as it should among indigenous sources, in part because the field of multinational clandestine HUMINT is in its infancy. SIGINT also relies heavily on HUMINT for the emplacement of close-in technical monitoring devices, the procurement of listening posts, and the handling of real-time monitors and translators for close-in collection.

IMINT tends to be self-sufficient, but because of its genesis as a precision collection system with very high resolution, it still does not do wide-area surveillance. While IMINT still cannot see under jungle canopy, into caves, or even into urban areas in any sort of coherent manner, when told exactly where to look, IMINT can add value. The advent of UAVs has dramatically increased IMINT value at the tactical level, but the processing and the connection from the collection platform to the end-user in the field are still severely deficient.

MASINT depends heavily on HUMINT for collecting samples (e.g., of water downstream from a suspected bio-chemical factory) or for emplacing close-in devices that seek to collect signatures in the form of smells, air composition, or other electro-magnetic anomalies characteristic of specific capabilities.

Cyberwar, both offensive cyberwar and defensive cybersecurity, is in its infancy, the warnings and the substantive recommendations of the early 1990s having been ignored. The importance of HUMINT in cyberwar cannot be overstated, but will certainly be ignored by the new "cyber czar." Both offensive and defensive CI—HUMINT subdisciplines—should play a major role in both defensive protection and offensive penetration of cyberspace.

All four of the mentioned above technical collection disciplines should, but do not, rely heavily on OSINT. Although the NSA has a fine effort to leverage OSINT in targeting telecommunications (for example, using OSINT to study the emergent Chinese cellular capabilities), and the National Geospatial-Intelligence Agency (NGA) makes use of commercial source imagery, in reality both the NSA and the NGA are so heavily defined by their legacy systems that they have yet to make the fullest possible use of OSINT in all languages and mediums. MASINT is very new and has sought to leverage OSINT, but MASINT relies too heavily on defense contractors (very large vendors), and the latter are not skilled at global OSINT in all languages using HUMINT intermediaries—they prefer to sell the government "butts in seats" surfing the Internet, a means of running up very large bills (and 200 percent overhead charges) without actually drilling down to exactly what is needed and could be obtained at very low cost if they truly understood multinational open sources and methods.

Remembering that OSINT is a part of HUMINT, Figure 7 illustrates how OSINT should be managed, both to relieve the classified disciplines of requirements that can be answered with open sources and methods, and to enhance the efficacy of the classified sources and methods.

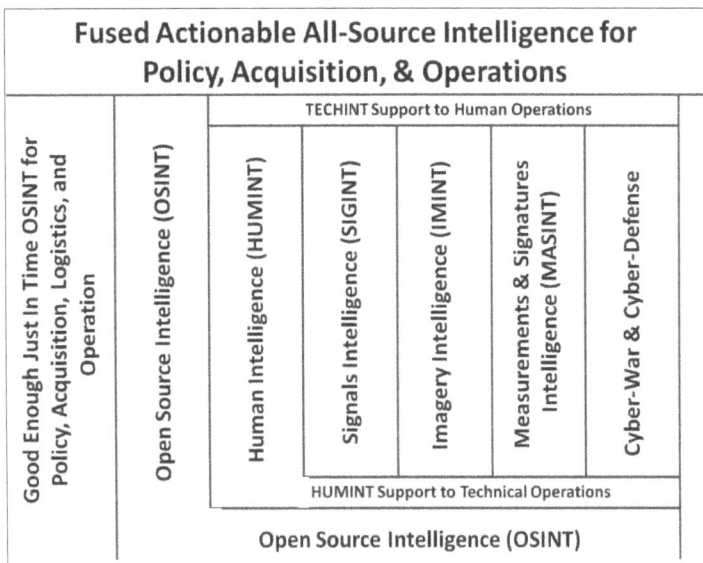

Figure 7. OSINT andClassified HUMINT in Relation to Other INTs.

CONCLUSION: THE HUMINT PLAYING FIELD

General Gray created the MCIA because he understood that expeditionary and constabulary operations were unique, and that intelligence support for the USMC was not to be had from others. I now believe that HUMINT must be elevated to be the "first service" (inclusive of OSINT) and that the intelligence directors or advisors to agency heads, cabinet secretaries, and commanders, among others, must be, above all, skilled at HUMINT requirements definition and consumption, as well as sharing all information they touch on their own. Figure 8 illustrates integrating the three main consumer groups and the 10 threats and 12 policies they must address, while also depicting the internal HUMINT capabilities, the external HUMINT network of "eight tribes," and the M4IS2 environment.

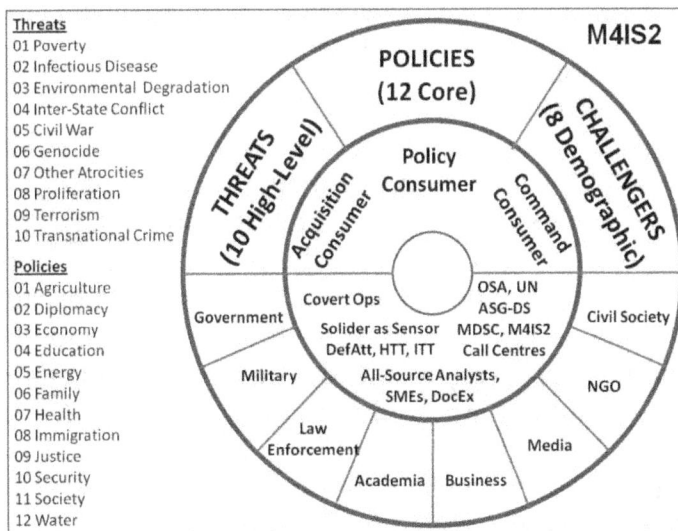

Figure 8. HUMINT Field—Sources, Targets, and Consumers.

The military is responsible for defending against all threats, not just armed threats. I believe that the Republic is facing serious threats to its survival, threats both domestic and foreign, and that the DoD and the DIA must rise to these challenges if we are to preserve and protect the United States in the 21st century.

HUMINT and Whole of Government Force Structure.

I have participated in two force structure studies and written a number of chapters and articles on strategy and force structure.[124] The guidance of Senator Sam Nunn (D-GA) remains eternally valuable:

> I am constantly being asked for a bottom-line defense number. I don't know of any logical way to arrive at such a figure without analyzing the threat; without determining what changes in our strategy should be made in light of the changes in the threat; and then determining what force structure and weapons programs we need to carry out this revised strategy.[125]

HUMINT must strive to meet the needs of all consumers across all agencies of government, in large part because the civilian successes help avoid a need for the military interventions and mobilizations; and because the future is unaffordable as things now stand. The United States is insolvent, the government is chaotically incoherent, and only intelligence-driven leadership can save us. General Gray nailed it in 1988, listing the differences between conventional and emerging threats (see Figure 9):[126]

Conventional Threat	Emerging Threat
Governmental	Nongovernmental
Conventional/Nuclear	Nonconventional (Assymmetric)
Static Orders of Battle (OOB)	Dynamic or Random OOB
Linear Development	Non-linear (e.g., Off the Shelf)
Rules of Engagement (ROE)	No Constraints (ROE)
Known Doctrine	Unknown Doctrine
Strategic Warning	No Established Intelligence and Warning Network
Known Intelligence Assets	Unlimited 5th Column

Figure 9. Déjà vu — The USMC Knew All This in 1988 (21 Years Ago).

In 1998 the U.S. Army Strategy Conference addressed force structure needs. Figure 10 is a depiction of the "Four Forces After Next" that I presented in 1998 to general acceptance.[127] In 2008, the same an-nual conference addressed the same question, the findings in 1998 having been ignored, and we have yet to see any grasp of whole of government strategic planning and programming from the White House, the OMB, or the Cabinet Secretaries.[128]

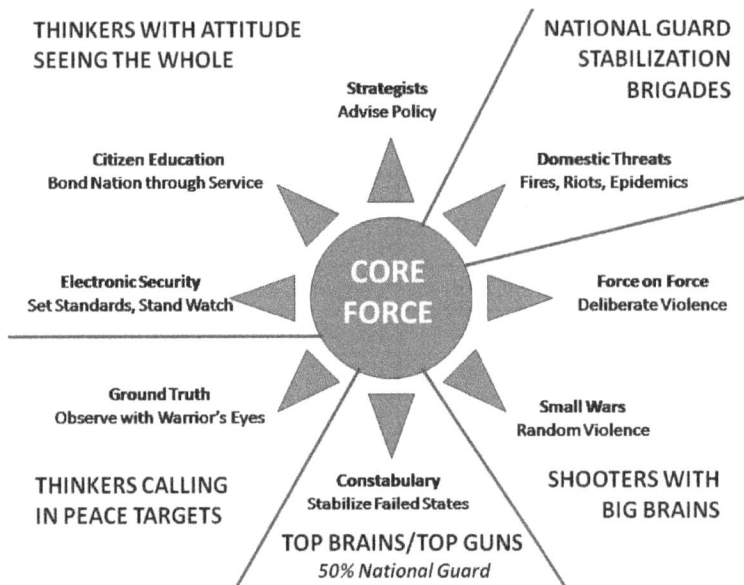

THINKERS WITH ATTITUDE
SEEING THE WHOLE

Strategists
Advise Policy

NATIONAL GUARD
STABILIZATION
BRIGADES

Citizen Education
Bond Nation through Service

Domestic Threats
Fires, Riots, Epidemics

Electronic Security
Set Standards, Stand Watch

CORE FORCE

Force on Force
Deliberate Violence

Ground Truth
Observe with Warrior's Eyes

Small Wars
Random Violence

THINKERS CALLING
IN PEACE TARGETS

Constabulary
Stabilize Failed States

SHOOTERS WITH
BIG BRAINS

TOP BRAINS/TOP GUNS
50% National Guard

Figure 10. DoD as a HUMINT Force for Peace, Security, and M4IS2.

Now is the time for the President and Secretary of Defense to think "big."[129]

Only the DoD can move, deliver, and communicate globally on a no-notice basis, and this is why the DoD should be the core force for all future whole of government operations. This is a concept I developed in the 1990s for a briefing to East and West European parliamentarians at the George Marshall Center, a concept I continue to believe in, that prizes the DoD as the hub of interagency operations, both domestically and internationally. It merits comment that three of the core force elements are thinkers rather than shooters, three are shooters able to think, and the last—constabulary stabilization operations—is an even mix of thinkers and shooters.

I will not belabor Sun Tzu's wisdom about the acme of skill being victory without fighting, but I will point out that the PRC is waging peace (irregular warfare) with presidential-level trade missions, massive loans, major construction projects, and free headquarters buildings for regional organizations (no extra charge for the embedded audio-visual remote monitoring devices). They have also mastered cyber warfare, something I and others warned about in the early 1990s.[130]

From where I sit, the USG is scattered, and only the DoD can get us on track. Figure 11 shows my 1998 depiction of the "Four Forces After Next," updated to show the IO implications.

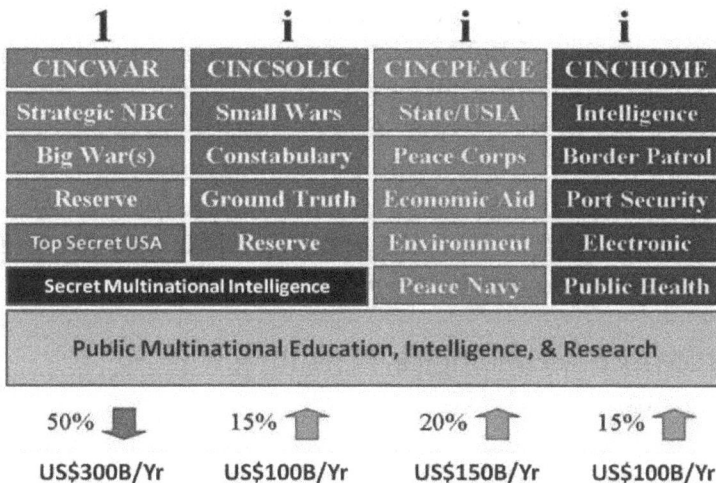

1	i	i	i
CINCWAR	CINCSOLIC	CINCPEACE	CINCHOME
Strategic NBC	Small Wars	State/USIA	Intelligence
Big War(s)	Constabulary	Peace Corps	Border Patrol
Reserve	Ground Truth	Economic Aid	Port Security
Top Secret USA	Reserve	Environment	Electronic
Secret Multinational Intelligence		Peace Navy	Public Health
Public Multinational Education, Intelligence, & Research			

50% ⬇	15% ⬆	20% ⬆	15% ⬆
US$300B/Yr	US$100B/Yr	US$150B/Yr	US$100B/Yr

+ SOLIC = Special Operations and Low Intensity Conflict.
+ Cost of National Guard redirection split amoung all four CINCS.
+ CINCHOME Intelligence includes citizen continuing education.

Figure 11. Four Forces After Next with IO Attributes.

I venture to suggest that the CIA is never going to offer whole of government intelligence suitable for deciding how we train, equip, and organize both military and civilian elements of the USG. In fairness, the DoD does not use intelligence properly to support all policymakers, all acquisition managers, or all commanders, staff, and action officers across the interagency spectrum of need, but there is no reason why it cannot do so beginning immediately. It merits comment that because of the size of its budget—the largest discretionary spending element in the total USG budget—how the DoD applies intelligence really makes a huge difference. If the DoD commits to nonfossil fuels (which also have very low heat signatures), it can move an entire industry overnight. Similarly, what the DoD does in the way of personnel policies impacts on the whole nation. I believe we need to restore universal service, but with a huge difference—only volunteers are joined to the Armed Forces and the Peace Corps, all others are directed into homeland duties.[131]

If the DoD will take the lead with respect to most if not all of HUMINT, we all win. A Nation's best defense is an educated citizenry.

HUMINT Technologies—Enabling Not Defining HUMINT.

Where HUMINT has been failed by the information technology (IT) function is with respect to desktop analytics and very large-scale processing. Today, the very best office I know is J-23 at U.S. Special Operations Command (USSOCOM), and they are still having to deal with over 20 distinct software packages that no one has been able to integrate.[132] If we shift to F/OSS, as many governments are doing, this will help.

As we move into multinational HUMINT operations, we will encounter a need to share very large databases with very strong encryption, as well as geospatial attributes, and we will need to do this at machine speed.

I believe the next revolution in HUMINT will be found in helping both overt and covert analysts and operators to connect the dots in the first two phases of the HUMINT cycle; spotting and assessing, while also exploiting much more ably all that comes from the handling phase of the HUMINT cycle.[133]

Multinational information-sharing and sense-making is going to be the primary means by which we add value to both shared and unilateral HUMINT. Near-real-time M4IS2 is the center of gravity, NOT unilateral operations.

One technology and its application that has impressed me greatly is biometrics. Used to anonymously identify sources prone to selling their knowledge to multiple buyers, it may prove to be the most sensational deconfliction device around, and can be scaled to allow for multinational source deconfliction along with visualization of multinational networks of sources relevant to any given geospatial area of interest or topical domain.

We can do better on hand-held reporting devices with embedded encryption, as well as at-rest encrypted storage of anything that leaves a secure facility.

Human-emplaced sensors, including disposable sensors that melt down in 24 hours, as well as brown-water electronic picket lines, are of interest to me. The ability to sense explosives regardless of the container, something I identified as a requirement for the Marine Corps in 1988, remains unmet.[134]

Telelanguage, mentioned earlier, and regional information-sharing and sense-making centers can double as call centers for secure calls from the street (a global Early Warning network no government can afford, that is on 24/7), should allow for tactical real-time document exploitation as well as tactical real-time translation of any dialect, 24/7, no matter where one is in the world.

HUMINT can and should be applied to IT discovery and development.[135]

HUMINT: The Essence of the Republic, of Defense, of the U.S. Army.

American national security has been severely undermined by decades of excessive spending on strategic technologies at the expense of tactical human-centered technologies; by a lack of integrity (or more kindly, perspective) across the board among our executive and legislative branch leaders; by a confusion between loyalty to the Constitution (we swear an oath to defend it) and loyalty to the chain of command; and by information asymmetries and data pathologies that have prevented the art and science of intelligence— decision-support—from developing.[136]

I believe that HUMINT, properly understood, is about education, intelligence, and research in the public interest. HUMINT is predominantly overt, and to the extent that overt HUMINT is properly managed, clandestine HUMINT and covert HUMINT, as well as both defensive and offensive counterintelligence, can be ethical, precise, and consequential.

George Will once published a collection of his Op Ed pieces under the title, *Statecraft as Soulcraft*.[137] I firmly believe that HUMINT is the pinnacle of the intelligence profession, for it deals with the most gloriously complex, challenging, and potentially enlightened (now most dangerous) species on the Earth.

HUMINT has spent the last quarter-century being displaced by the technical collection disciplines in
every sense of the word but one: results. One good
HUMINT asset, whether overt or covert, is worth
more and costs less than any constellation of complex
technologies whose product cannot be processed in a
timely fashion, and that requires tens of thousands of
human beings to create, maintain, and exploit.

America today needs multiple forms of healing,
from how we elect our leaders to how we govern
ourselves, to how we preserve and protect the Republic. In every single instance, it will be HUMINT, not
some arcane collection of technologies, that discovers,
discriminates, distills, and delivers education, intelligence (decision support), and research—whether
from direct human observation or with support from
technologies—for the benefit of humanity.

Machines are programmed and perform at the
lowest common denominator of the sum of their human contributors. Humans, in contrast—properly led,
properly trained, properly equipped—are uniquely
capable of "on the fly" innovation, catalytic insights,
nuanced expression, compassionate listening, and a
myriad of other tradecraft as well as socio-cultural
skills that no machine will ever master.

*HUMINT is the essence of the Republic, and "only
integrity is going to count."*[139] *Integrity. E Veritate Po-
tens (From Truth, Power).*

WHAT HAS CHANGED?

I thought to conclude with two charts, and then
offer some recommendations for the future direction
of U.S. Army HUMINT. Figure 12 shows the old standard Principles of War (with their acrostic MOOSE-

MUSS), with the traditional definitions on the left and the modern alternative definitions on the right.

M – Mass – Concentrate Combat Power at decisive time and place.	Mass: the aggregate commons sense of the public, sharing wisdom
O – Objective – Direct every military operation against a clearly defined, decisive and obtainable objective.	Objective: the collective good achieved through appreciative inquiry, and sustainable precisely because it reflects group consensus
O – Offensive – Seize, retain and exploit the initiative.	Offensive: neutralize any attack with swarm offense and dissipation defense.
S – Surprise – Strike the enemy at a time, a place and in a manner for which he is unprepared.	Surprise is for the stupid. Cast a wide net, put enough eyes and ears on it, and no bug is invisible.
E - Economy of Force – Allocate minimum combat power to secondary efforts.	Expansion of Force: here comes everybody, an Army of Davids, the network is the computer
M - Maneuver - Place the enemy in a position of disadvantage through flexible application of combat power.	Maneuver to have no enemies, but instead to create infinite stabilizing wealth and robust communities
U - Unity of Command – For every objective, ensure unity of effort under one responsible commander.	Unity of Purpose within all groups and at all levels (local, provincial, national, regional global) is the only sure deal
S – Security – Never permit the enemy to acquire an unexpected advantage.	Security "just in case" is evil and expensive; the best security comes from good intention & trust building
S – Simplicity – Prepare clear, uncomplicated plans and clear, concise orders to ensure understanding.	Sensibility is the root of all good – if it makes sense, others will agree; if it does not, you should not be doing it

Figure 12. Principles of War versus Principles of Peace.

When combined with the 10 high-level threats to humanity that Dr. Brent Scowcroft, Lieutenant General USAF (Ret.), and others defined in the report of the High-Level Panel on Threats, Challenges, and Opportunities, we cannot help but observe that the current U.S. national security strategy ignores all but two of these threats. Some opportunities for the U.S. Army are identified in Figure 13.

High-Level Threat	US Army Opportunities
Poverty	Stability Guarantees for Demilitarization
	Civil Affairs Brigade as Cadre for Global Army
Infectious Disease	National Guard medical at home & abroad
	Universal draft & culture of fitness
	Healthy environmental standards for all
	National Guard as natural cure data source
Environmental Degradation	Precision intervention & reconstruction
	Rapid response disaster relief
Inter-State Conflict	Free cell phones and connectivity to all
	Free knowledge on demand in all languages
	Global Range of Gifts Table to house level
Civil War	End U.S. support for the 42 dictators we love
	End overseas bases and deployments
	Focus on peaceful preventive measures
Genocide	End small arms trade as SOF interdiction
Other Atrocities	Global biometrics to stop trade in humans
	Screen and do not train gang members
Proliferation	End U.S. role as world's #1 merchant of death
	Regional small arms interdiction networks
Terrorism (Large Scale)	Flag officer integrity — keep eye on the ball
	Use Rangers to interdict bin Ladens
	Regional harmonization of efforts
	Tactical excellence in "track & whack"[i]
Transnational Organized Crime	Create international law enforcement cadre
	Use Rangers to take down key nodes

Figure 13. Summary of Threat Opportunities for U.S. Army.

"Unclassified decision support to all parties" has been removed from each of the blocks above, in part to emphasize that it is the foundation for everything the U.S. Army might seek to do, and therefore must become as pervasive and ingrained in every concept and doctrine so as to redefine the U.S. Army as the world's first information operations (IO) force in being.

RECOMMENDATIONS

Embracing the U.S. Army as a whole person organization, the following recommendations are intended to both create a smart Army that is globally mobile and effective, while also making the U.S. Army the single most effective hub for both interagency whole of government operations, and multinational multifunctional operations.

1. **Civil Affairs Command**. I recommend that Civil Affairs be upgraded to at least a three-star command but ideally a four-star command that embraces military police, medical, engineering, and other human-to-human specializations, retaining the regional structure but creating regional brigades in which the U.S. battalion is the core force for a multinational brigade that includes nongovernmental and other nonmilitary force structure. Psychological Operations (PSYOP) is long over-due for being phased out. A new blend of strategic communications and OSINT could be developed under the Civil Affairs Information Management rubric, with decision support and multinational information-sharing as a primary mission area.

2. **Global Health**. The United States is completely lacking in domestic surge capacity across the board. There is an urgent need for field hospitals and mobile medical units that can be deployed on a worldwide basis to contain diseases that might otherwise jump on an airplane and come home; these capabilities would also be structured for rapid redeployment to the home front as needed.

3. **Environmental Engineering**. The Corps of Engineers can be brought into the 21st century and made a globally-potent force if its culture can be modified and humanized. Poverty creates more environmental damage and more disease and more crime than any natural disaster, at the same time that most natural disasters are actually acts of man (e.g., paving over watersheds, thus increasing the virulence of storms). Sustainable design is the combat zone of the future. Just as the Army needs strategists, so does it need engineers capable of Earth engineering.

4. **Communications**. Nokia has developed cell phones that recharge on ambient energy and do not need an electrical grid in support. We are at the very beginning of an era where face-to-face human communications are the acme of skill, and vastly more important than force of arms for the simple reason that there are not enough guns on the planet to force our way. Communications educate, education creates stabilizing wealth. Crowded spectrum is an issue right now. The U.S. Army could take the lead in devising open spectrum communications and fielding a multi-national Communications Corps working in tandem with the Civil Affairs Corps to free individuals from ideologues by giving them the means to "jack-in" to the global grid directly.

5. **Logistics**. We cannot afford to meet the needs of the five billion poor, but we can offer the world a Global Range of Needs Table that leverages other people's time and money. In tandem, the Civil Affairs Corps and the Communications Corps could make it possible for one trillion dollars a year of funds from organizations, as well as the one billion rich (80 percent of whom do not give to charity now), to voluntarily harmonize their programs and spending, while

individuals use Army-documented needs online to do peer-to-peer giving. There are some programs now that do this, all tiny. A global grid is needed, and the U.S. Army can offer it up as a spin-off of its global ground-truth observations.

6. **Biometrics**. In my view, the greatest threat to the internal stability and the long-term effectiveness of the U.S. Army is the raw fact that it is training the Taliban in Afghanistan and criminal gang members in the United States. A global effort is needed to create a biometric database of every person of interest who should *not* be trained by the U.S. Army, and who should *not* be admitted to a Western country. Mobile teams from the U.S. Army can install and service these devices while surveying law enforcement capabilities.

7. **Track and Whack**. The carpet bombing approach to community neutralization does not work. The U.S. Army is perfectly suited to develop a global multinational "track and whack" program that is legitimized by an international court and includes internationally-posted convictions and demands for surrender followed by "one man-one bullet" administration of punitive and preventive justice. This cannot be done outside of international law. It *must* have global legal validity.

ENDNOTES

1. Dr. Joseph Markowitz, the first and only Director of the Community Open Source Program Office (COSPO), and I have agreed that it is vital to distinguish among open source information (OSIF), open source intelligence (OSINT), and validated OSINT (OSINT-V), the latter of which can only be done by government all-source analysts with full access to all relevant Top Secret CODEWORD information. In this monograph, OSINT represents all three, the distinctions having been made in this

note. A recent discussion about misperceptions in OSINT is contained in "The Open Source Program: Missing in Action," *International Journal of Intelligence and Counterintelligence*, Fall 2008, pp. 609-619, available from *www.phibetaiota.net/?p=2603*.

2. Further on in this monograph, I quote General Anthony Zinni, USMC (Ret.), as saying that secret sources provided "at best" 4 percent of his command knowledge. I believe that the 80-20 rule of thumb is a good one with respect to just about anything, but the reality is that no more than 10 percent of what we need to know to do strategic, operational, tactical, and technical intelligence is actually secret and worth the risk of going after—two different things.

3. For the sake of brevity and because the U.S. Army is the "center of gravity" for what few advances are taking place in the related fields of communications, education, and intelligence, the term "Soldier" is used in this monograph to represent all individuals on the cutting edge of danger in the service of their country, i.e., it includes Soldiers, Sailors, Marines, Airmen, members of the Coast Guard, and police on the beat in every neighborhood.

4. For close to a decade, I have been saying $65 billion, deliberately understated, while the official number slipped to the public by Mary Graham, then Deputy Director of National Intelligence for Collection (DDNI/C) has been $44 billion. We know now that the actual amount is at least $75 billion, as announced by the current Director of National Intelligence (DNI), Admiral Dennis Blair, USN (Ret.), on September 15, 2009, reported in Adam Entous, "Secretive Spending on U.S. Intelligence Disclosed," *Reuters*, Tuesday, September 15, 2009, available from *www.phibetaiota.net/?p=10778*. This number does not factor in certain other programs in Treasury and Defense to which the DNI is probably not privy.

5. General Zinni's complete quotation to this effect is found on p. 15.

6. In the intelligence world, "discipline" refers to one of the major forms of collection—human, imagery, signals, and measurements and signatures—while in the academic world, discipline refers to a specialization topic such as archeology, history,

or psychology. I use the term multidisciplinary to refer to both, and will further discuss the unusual complexity that emerges when one deals with all that humans can know in all forms about all topics.

7. My seminal article, also briefed by invitation to the Library of Congress Forum, is "Creating a Smart Nation: Strategy, Policy, Intelligence, and Information," *Government Information Quarterly*; Vol. 13 No. 2, pp. 159-173; and "Creating a Smart Nation: Information Strategy, Virtual Intelligence, and Information Warfare," in Doug Dearth, Alan Campen, and R. Thomas Goodden, contributing eds., *CYBERWAR: Security, Strategy, and Conflict in the Information Age*, Fair Oaks, VA: Armed Forces Communications and Electronics Association (AFCEA), May 1996. Later I created the book, *THE SMART NATION ACT: Public Intelligence in the Public Interest*, Oakton, VA: OSS, 2006, which provides all necessary information to actually implement these ideas.

8. PriceWaterhouseCoopers has documented the fact that over 50 percent of every dollar spent on health care in the United States is wasted, available from *blogs.wsj.com/health/2008/04/10/report-us-wastes-more-than-half-of-health-spending/*. The USG is an industrial-era system that has been captured by special interests. It combines industrial-era legions of clerks with top-down micromanagement, and in the worst of all possible worlds, misspends the bulk of the taxpayer dollar. At the same time, it seeks to restrict and preempt state and local governments in their legitimate setting of higher public standards for the environment and other areas; instead, the federal government now sets ceilings rather than floors, and this is the truth-teller on the failure of the existing government to adapt and to maintain its integrity.

9. See Senate Floor Statement on Secretary Robert Gates' speech on "Tools of Persuasion and Inspiration," July 28, 2008, available from *www.levin.senate.gov/newsroom/release.cfm?id=301378*.

10. As identified in priority order by the United Nations High-Level Panel on Threats, Challenges, and Change in their report, *A More Secure World: Our Shared Responsibility*, New York: United Nations, 2004.

11. I served as the Special Assistant to the Director (GM-14) and also as the Deputy Director, a gapped billet for a lieutenant colonel. Colonel Walter Breede III, USMC, was my first boss; Colonel Forest Lucy, USMC, my second; and I consider them, along with Colonel Vincent Stewart, USMC, to be three of the finest Marine colonels I have known in my lifetime. Their leadership has made a huge difference in my professional life.

12. Wikipedia provides an adequate summary entitled *Nicaragua v. United States*, available from *en.wikipedia.org/wiki/Nicaragua_v._United_States*.

13. Sherman Kent, *Strategic Intelligence for American World Policy*, Princeton, NJ: Princeton University Press, 1949. The single best description I have found of the CIA's loss of integrity during and after the Vietnam war can be found in C. Michael Hiam's utterly brilliant *Who the Hell Are We Fighting?: The Story of Sam Adams and the Vietnam Intelligence Wars*, Hanover, NH: Steerforth Press, 2006, where he quotes Kent asking Adams if the CIA's complicity in not counting the guerrillas (the Viet Cong) was "beyond the bounds of reasonable dishonesty." p. 122. His work is complemented by many other books, notably George Allen's *None So Blind: A Personal Account of the Intelligence Failure in Vietnam*, New York: Ivan R. Dee, 2001; Bruce Jones, *War Without Windows*, Berkeley, CA: Berkeley University Press, 1990; Jim Wirtz, *The Tet Offensive: Intelligence Failure in War*, Ithaca, NY: Cornell University Press, 1994; and Orrin de Forest, *Slow Burn: The Rise and Bitter Fall of American Intelligence in Vietnam*, New York: Simon & Schuster, 1990. More recently, after visiting the CIA, John Perry Barlow actually described the environment he experienced as a "gulag," in "Why Spy: If the spooks can't analyze their own data, why call it intelligence?" *Forbes ASAP*, October 7, 2002, available from *www.forbes.com/asap/2002/1007/042.html*.

14. The short version of the modern contest of will, intellect, and integrity between the CIA and me is available from *www.oss.net/HISTORY*.

15. See Rowan Scarborough, "Tenet's House of Cards," *Human Events .com*, August 23, 2007, available from *www.humanevents.com/article.php?id=22063*.

16. As identified by the Earth Intelligence Network (EIN) from a review of Mandate for Change volumes for the last five presidential elections in the USA. They are: agriculture, diplomacy, economy, education, energy, family, health, immigration, justice, security, society, and water. It makes no sense, for example, to use water to grow grain we cannot eat to fuel cars that either should not be built at all, or should be running on natural gas from Alaska.

17. Having authored four books specifically focused on the reinvention of intelligence, I will only point to my most recent works that address the larger context for intelligence reinvention beyond HUMINT. They include "Intelligence for the President — AND Everyone Else," *CounterPunch*, February 27-March 1, 2009; "Fixing the White House and the Intelligence Community," White Paper, *OSS.Net*, January 15, 2009; "The New Craft for Peacekeeping Intelligence," in *Information and Intelligence Cooperation in Multifunctional International Organizations*, Stockholm, Sweden: Folke Bernadotte Academy Sweden, March 30-April 7, 2009; and "The Ultimate Hack: Re-Inventing Intelligence to Re-Engineer Earth," Denmark, October 27-28, 2009, available from *www.oss. net/HACK*. Also relevant is my 3-day training for the "Class Before One" comprised of six UN system elements in a wartorn country, "Creating the United Nations Open-Source Decision-Support Information Network (UNODIN)," August 2007. My 1990s evaluation of the CIA, "HUMINT Successes & Failures," is still valid and available from *www.phibetaiota.net/?p=3601*.

18. This quote has been confirmed by the Library of Congress and the University of Virginia as attributable to Thomas Jefferson. Benjamin Franklin. "Humanity Ascending" is a phrase I learned from Barbara Marx Hubbard, and the DVD series by the same title. She cited Benjamin Franklin's reference to the "divinity in our humanity." HUMINT is not about spying. HUMINT is about learning, deciding, and evolving — humanity ascending.

19 "Private Enterprise Intelligence: Its Potential Contribution to National Security," *Intelligence and National Security*, Vol. 10, No. 4, October 1995. The concept of both the journal and the book that followed, were presented at the 1994 conference sponsored

by the Canadian Association for Security and Intelligence Studies (CASIS).

20. Searching for "Valley of Death" defense acquisition will yield the latest articles. As of this writing, the best available is from the *Government Executive*.

21. The best observation Chuck Spinney (the leading defense whistleblower in the 1980s) ever made to me was in November 2008, when we had lunch, and he pointed out that not only does the DoD research influence, define, and overpower most research funded within the United States, but the most pernicious effect has been to raise multiple generations of engineers trained to do "government specifications, cost plus" engineering, which is to say, the worst possible solutions at the greatest possible cost. In the private sector, biomimicry and "cradle to cradle" zero waste engineering are flourishing at a time when defense is so bogged down in 1950s mind-sets and 1970s contract vehicles that it is lucky it has not collapsed completely. This cannot stand – it must be transformed.

22. "The only way to understand a system is to understand the system it fits into." Howard Odum was a pioneer of systems ecology. Phi Beta Iota, the Public Intelligence Blog (*www.phibeta-iota.net*), is a standard reference site now.

23. The Army Strategy Conference in 1998 produced the first coherent vision for "what next" but was ignored. In 2008, the same conference addressed the need to rebalance the instruments of national power, and this too is being ignored despite the fact that the Director of National Intelligence (DNI) has been, up to this point, a major proponent of national security reform. We do not lack for knowledge – what we lack is access for those with knowledge to those in power. Lip service, theater, and incrementalism are in no way transformative. "Perhaps We Should Have Shouted: A Twenty-Year Retrospective," available from *www. phibetaiota.net/?p=5818*.

24. Government; military; law enforcement; academia; business; media; nonprofit and nongovernmental; and civil society inclusive of labor unions, religions, and citizen advocacy groups as well as emergent citizen wisdom councils.

25. My tentative view on how the USG and DoD could do this is at my briefing for engineers, "The Ultimate Hack: Re-Inventing Intelligence to Re-Engineer Earth", available from *www.phibetaiota.net/?CA5=114.*

26. Senator Sam Nunn (D-GA) remains the most cogent thinker on this point. At the time (1991 or 1992), Senator Nunn was Chairman of the Senate Armed Services Committee (SASC). I copied down these words of wisdom while serving in the C4I Division of HQMC as the General Defense Intelligence Program (GDIP) analyst. I have never been able to locate the original reference again, but in direct correspondence with Senator Nunn's staff in his retirement, they said it sounded right. I have used this quote before, but it evidently has never registered with any Secretary of Defense:

> I am continually being asked for a bottom-line defense number. I don't know of any logical way to arrive at such a figure without analyzing the threat; without determining what changes in our strategy should be made in light of the changes in the threat; and then determining what force structure and weapons programs we need to carry out this revised strategy.

> I know with absolute certainty that the Secretary of Defense knows the answer at an intellectual level — anything I can do, he can do better — but at a bureaucratic level, he is not asking the right question, which is: In light of what we now know about the threat (see below), how should we change the totality of the federal, state, and local governments, and the totality of the eight tribes that comprise any nation, so as to achieve Buckminster Fuller's vision? His core question and his reflection on war on politics:

> How can we make the world work for 100 percent of humanity in the shortest possible time through spontaneous cooperation without ecological damage or disadvantage to anyone?

Either you're going to go along with your mind and the truth, or you're going to yield to fear and custom and conditioned reflexes. With our minds alone we can discover those principles we need to employ to convert all humanity to success in a new, harmonious relationship with the universe. We have the option to make it.

Since it is now physically and metaphysically demonstrable that the chemical elemental resources of Earth already mined or in recirculation, plus the knowledge we now have, are adequate to the support of all humanity and can be feasibly redesign-employed to support all humanity at a higher standard of living than ever before enjoyed by any human, war is now and henceforth murder. All weapons are invalid. Lying is intolerable. All politics are not only obsolete but lethal. Available from *www.newworldencyclopedia.org/entry/Buckminster_Fuller*.

Now imagine if 50 percent of the Defense Advanced Research Project Agency's (DARPA) budget were redirected to waging peace — instead of robots programmed in theory to not commit war crimes; why not very low cost solutions for clean water, renewable energy, disease eradication, and so on? DARPA represents the best and the brightest engineers lacking inspired leadership and global perspective. Winning wars is not an outcome — creating a sustainable peace is.

We still need spies and secrecy, we still need "four forces after next" to deter and win wars, but more than anything else we need intelligence-driven policy, acquisition, and operations, whole of government policy, acquisition, and operations, and most especially, whole of government integrity. Show me that, and I will show you a prosperous world at peace.

Fifty-two questions and answers suitable for the President of the United States are easily available from the Earth Intelligence Network, *www.earth-intelligence.net*. It says a great deal about a nation when those nominally responsible for the public interest are not asking these questions nor considering these answers (among other answers from other sources).

27. Max Weber, *The Theory of Social and Economic Organization*, New York: Free Press, 1997.

28. See "The Ultimate Hack: Re-Inventing Intelligence to Re-Engineer Earth."

29. Action officers (AO) today are one deep and have zero resources for securing OSINT, nor do they receive any support at all from the USIC. In the Department of Energy (DoE), to take one example, the AO for proliferation is in this situation, and despite the fact that the CIA has Carol Dumaine working at the DoE, the raw fact is that she is without influence or resources.

30. A major reason why the United States should pay for the Office of the Assistant Secretary General for Decision Support in the UN is so as to obtain UN validation of the table, which can be presented to all foundations and others at an annual conference. By allowing anyone to add a peace target at all levels (from household and village needs to a regional need for a water desalination plant), we harness the minds — and wallets — of every human on the planet. Peer-to-peer giving, not foundation giving, is going to save the world by elevating the poor to the point that they can create infinite wealth. For a graphic depiction of how an online Global Range of Needs Table would work, see my briefing, "The Ultimate Hack, Re-Inventing Intelligence to Re-Engineer Earth."

31. There is no substitute for having a high-quality HUMINT professional alongside every major consumer of intelligence. Requirements Definition is easily one third of the value of the intelligence profession, the other two being Collection Management inclusive of source discovery and discrimination; and Analytic Tradecraft which should but does not now include advanced IT exploitation of all available information.

32. The obvious reference is to H. G. Wells, *World Brain*, London, UK: Adamantine Press, 1993. See also Howard Bloom, *Global Brain: The Evolution of Mass Mind from the Big Bang to the 21st Century*, New York: Wiley, 2001; and Hans Swegan, *Global Mind*, London, UK: Minerva Press, 1995.

33. Medard Gabel, co-creator with Buckminster Fuller of the analog World Game, is the architect for the EarthGame™ which

is not really a game at all, but rather an interactive *Operating Manual for Spaceship Earth* as he and Buckminster Fuller originally envisioned. The preliminary planning documents are available from *www.phibetaiota.net/?p=14031*.

34. My own examination of *The Foreign Affairs System of the People's Republic of China*, Bethlehem, PA: Lehigh University, 1975, remains quite valid and is available online in my Early Papers. A current and concise definition of the "five circles" of Iranian HUMINT has been provided by Amir Taheri, "As the U.S. Retreats, Iran Fills the Void," *Wall Street Journal*, May 4, 2009. The five circles are (1) commercial companies and banks, many of them fronts; (2) charities and scholarships; (3) cultural centers offering language and religion; (4) Hezbollah operating openly; and (5) clandestine operations with and without indigenous Sunni radicals in support. For an overview of Iran's penetration of Latin America, see Samuel Logan, "Iran's Inroads and Deepening Ties in Latin America," *Mexidata.info*, May 4, 2009, including the phrase "as Iran continues to strengthen relationships, more Iranian doctors, diplomats, teachers, businessmen and officials are arriving in Latin America."

35. They appear to be further trisected into Service, command, and tactical capabilities. As the global grid is enhanced, these distinctions will become impediments, and it will be necessary to harness all humans into one adaptable matrix. There also appear to be a number of subterfuges for obscuring some units in order to avoid their being subject to oversight, just as some acquisitions are mislabeled, e.g., hand-held devices as code for special lap-top computers.

36. While my observations are probably applicable to every government and every nation, I limit my direct assertions to the USG and the USIC that I know, as well as to anyone now serving, tactical and technical details aside.

37. Education, lessons learned, research, and training (both planned and as needed) are the foundation for achieving organizational intelligence, which is Quadrant IV after knowledge management (KM), social networking (SN), and external research (ER). External research and development (ER&D) is for

all practical purposes dead within the IC and the DoD, less the spend-thrift DARPA and IC equivalents that are largely disconnected from the most urgent needs of the warfighter and intelligence professional. A depiction I first presented to the NSA at its first public conference in Las Vegas, NV, on January 9, 2002, is available from *www.phibetaiota.net/?p=21805*. I have chosen to use the terms defense counterintelligence and offensive counterintelligence instead of the DoD terms defensive counterespionage (DCE) and offensive counterespionage (OFCO) in part to specify that I am not addressing these more sensitive endeavors in any way, and in part to keep the terms more generic.

38. See Joe Bageant, *Deer Hunting with Jesus: Dispatches from America's Class War*, New York: Three Rivers Press, 2008.

39. See Gordon McKenzie, *Orbiting the Giant Hairball: A Corporate Fool's Guide to Surviving with Grace*, New York: Viking Adult, 1998. More recently, John Taylor Gatto, *Weapons of Mass Instruction*, Vancouver, British Columbia, Canada: New Society Publishers, 2008, has driven a definitive stake into the heart of the childhood extension and compulsory prison system we call school.

40. The anthroposphere is that part of the environment that is made or modified by humans for use in human activities and human habitats.

41. Noosphere, according to the thought of Vladimir Vernadsky and Teilhard de Chardin, denotes the "sphere of human thought."

42. Faith matters, both in terms of ensuring that ethics and integrity are present in all aspects of our professional and personal lives, and in a practical sense, as a common frame of reference in the practice of HUMINT. Religion has been neglected by HUMINT, and must be a priority for both mapping and understanding. I review a number of books on faith and religion at Phi Beta Iota, available from *www.phibetaiota.net*.

43. The OSA cannot be under the CIA or secret intelligence auspices for the simple reason that all of the information we want can be gotten for free from others, but only if the OSA is under

diplomatic auspices. The spies can have a copy of everything, but the original public information must remain public. See *Final Report of the National Commission on Terrorist Attacks Upon the United States*, Official Government Ed., Washington, DC: Government Printing Office, July 2004, pp. 23, 423.

44. See *Preparing for the 21st Century: An Appraisal of U.S. Intelligence*, Washington, DC: Government Printing Office, March 1996. A passing reference to the exercise is made in the section on "Improving Intelligence Analysis," subsection "Making Better Use of Open Sources," but the truthteller is in the final recommendation that OSINT be a top priority for both more funding and more attention from the (then) Director of Central Intelligence (DCI). Senator David Boren (D-OK), today President of the University of Oklahoma, was moved to contribute the foreword to my first book in part because — he says this in his foreword — both John Deutch and George Tenet refused to act on any of the recommendations of the Commission, and especially those recommendations regarding OSINT needing to be a top priority for funding and attention from the (then) DCI.

45. This, and other documents pertinent to the need for legislative resolution of the shortfalls in every presidential and congressional commission or panel on intelligence since 1947, is available from *www.oss.net/HILL*.

46. This must be a diplomatic organization because most organizations and individuals will not share information with an organization that is a formal part of the USIC, or even with the DoD. Led by a senior U.S. ambassador, it could be collocated with either the ASG for Decision Support at the UN, or the U.S. Mission to the UN.

47. Selfishly, this is the fastest means by which to orchestrate U.S. vacuum-cleaning of all unclassified information available from within the UN System. Pragmatically, by sponsoring a Global Range of Needs Table, this office would help multiple individuals and organizations collaborate (for example, a Rumanian engineer with a spare part needed in Ghana, a German willing to pay the FedEx fee, and a third party able to receive the part in the capital city and deliver it to the village needing the part). Thus, we harness the full human capacities of the planet; or help

organizations harmonize spending in a specific location such as East Timor (Timore-Leste).

48. There are a number of locations where an MDSC could be located, from Groton, CT, to New York to Quantico, VA, to Tampa, FL. I believe we have no alternative but to create the first de facto World Intelligence Center such as called for by Quincy Wright in the *Journal of Conflict Resolution* in 1957; and the sooner we do that, the sooner we can begin effectively harmonizing spending to create a prosperous world at peace through peaceful preventive measures.

49. This idea was first presented in the chapter on "Presidential Intelligence" in *ON INTELLIGENCE: Spies and Secrecy in an Open World*, Fair Oaks, VA: AFCEA, 2000. The National Intelligence University (NIU) that is part of the secret USIC is not suitable because its leaders know little about history, culture, language, or open sources of information, and they do not have the infrastructure for absorbing and enlightening large numbers of individuals not eligible for standard USIC clearances. The National Defense Intelligence College (NDIC) has done well with its Multinational Intelligence Fellows program, and this could be expanded as an immediate measure, but ultimately I believe we need to think in terms of a Multinational Multifunctional University in which six nations such as Brazil, China, India, South Africa, Turkey, and Russia offer 2-month segments, with the students moving from one to the other in sequence, and then spending a final 2 years in residence at the MDSC.

50. Since leaving government I have been a champion for reducing counterproductive secrecy while assuring necessary secrecy — as Rodney McDaniel, the Executive Secretary for the National Security Council has put it, only 10 percent of secrecy is actually legitimate, the rest is turf protection. As found in Thomas P. Croakley, ed., *Issues of Command and Control*, National Defense University, 1991, p. 68. My own testimony, in 1993, 1996, and 1997, has been very straightforward: Unnecessary secrecy impedes the effectiveness of government, while we also undermine our security with lip service to operations security (OPSEC) (e.g., clandestine operations run out of official installations where nothing can be kept secret including the identity of every single officer operating under official cover). I believe 20 percent of our secrecy is justified, but at least half of that is done badly.

51. U.S. Senate, *Commission on Protecting and Reducing Government Secrecy*, Document 105-2, Washington, DC: Government Printing Office, 1997. See also Ted Gup, *NATION OF SECRETS: The Threat to Democracy and the American Way of Life*, New York: Doubleday, 2007.

52. Read the letter of transmittal, available from *www.fas.org/sgp/library/moynihan/title.html*.

53. Arabic (11 core variations), Aramaic, Berber, Catelan, Chinese, Danish, Dari, Dutch, English, Farsi, Finnish, French, German, Hindi (a continuum of dialects), Indonesian, Irish, Italian, Japanese, Korean, Kurdish, Kurmanji, Malay, Norwegian, Pashto, Polish, Portuguese, Punjab, Russian, Serbian, Spanish, Swedish, Tamil, Turkish, and Urdu. Arabic variations (the CIA often falls prey to its dependence on Lebanese Arabs, and the FBI has similar issues): Andalusi Arabic (extinct, but has an important role in literary history); Egyptian Arabic (Egypt) considered the most widely understood and used "second dialect"; Gulf Arabic (Gulf coast from Kuwait to Oman, and minorities on the other side); Hassaniiya (in Mauritania); Hijazi Arabic; Iraqi Arabic; Leventine Arabic (Syrian, Lebanese, Palestinian, and western Jordanian); Maghreb Arabic (Tunisian, Algerian, Moroccan, and western Libyan); Maltese; Najdi Arabic; Sudanese Arabic (with a dialect continuum into Chad); and Yemeni Arabic.

54. I speculate that this refers in part to his ability to ask any of the 75+ nations participating in the Coalition Coordination Center (CCC) in Tampa, FL, for assistance. It is my view that the new fully-furnished CCC building should be converted into a Multinational Decision Support Center (MDSC) that can feed a copy of all unclassified documents into the high side of Intelink via the electronic loading docks already in existence at USSO-COM, while keeping ownership of the original so as to provide decision support to stabilization and reconstruction, humanitarian assistance, and disaster relief operations worldwide, all without being encumbered by specious claims from the secret world, which classifies *everything* for the simple reason that it only has one communications and computing mode: Top Secret/Sensitive Information. My briefing as given to the combined leaders of the

CCC delegations and then adapted for ASD/SOLIC (irregular warfare) is available from *www.oss.net/CCC*; I believe the center of gravity for HUMINT is both overt and civil, hence the new Army Civil Affairs Brigade and the UN need to become primary partners in collecting, processing, and exploiting of OSIF and OSINT.

55. General Zinni is quoted in my seminal chapter on strategic OSINT, "Open Source Intelligence," Loch D. Johnson, ed., *Strategic Intelligence Volume 2: The Intelligence Cycle*, Westport, CT: Praeger, 2007, pp. 95-122. The chapter alone is available from *www.oss.net/OSINT-S*. The operational counterpart to this, an updating of the *NATO Open Source Intelligence Handbook* that I wrote by direction of Brigadier General Jim Cox, CA (then Deputy J-2 for Supreme Allied Headquarters Europe) and with oversight from Lieutenant Commander Andrew Chester, CA, is in Loch Johnson, ed., *Handbook of Intelligence Studies*, Philadelphia, PA: Routledge, 2006, pp. 129-147. The chapter alone is available from *www.oss.net/OSINT-O*.

56. See "The Importance of Open Source Intelligence to the Military," Loch Johnson and James Wirtz, eds., *STRATEGIC INTELLIGENCE: Windows Into a Secret World*, Cary, NC: Roxbury, 2004, pp. 112-119, previously published in the *International Journal of Intelligence and Counterintelligence*. Winter 1995, pp. 457-470.

57. RapidSMS as pioneered by the United Nations Children's Fund (formerly United Nations International Children's Emergency Fund), is proving itself daily.

58. OSA would be the executive agent for this program. The National Guard can make a significant contribution — it is unique for being eligible for both military clearances to access secret national foreign intelligence, and law enforcement commissions from the Governor to allow access to crime databases. But the National Guard bureaucracy cannot be asked to manage an entirely new domestic program best funded and organized by the OSA and its interagency management team. I continue to believe that the National Guard, not the active duty force, should be reorganized into stabilization and reconstruction brigades to meet domestic needs and for short-term international needs with mili-

tary police, medical, legal, civil affairs, and other predominantly civil applications of organized forces.

59. See *www.oss.net/HILL* for more information.

60. Also as defined by the Earth Intelligence Network, on the basis of factual demographics: Brazil, China, India, Indonesia, Iran, Russia, Venezuela, and Wild Cards such as the Congo, Malaysia, South Africa, and Turkey.

61. Educating the poor "one cell call at a time" is the defining outcome and idea of the Earth Intelligence Network, and is described in the larger context of creating public intelligence in the public interest in a 10-page document. What most people do not realize is that the combination of free cell phones among the poor, when combined with call centers operated by the government, instantly comprise a national and regional early warning network without compare, and one unaffordable under any other schema.

62. Some quote this as ". . . all bugs are shallow." Regardless, the era of "open everything" is here to stay, and our task as intelligence professionals is to leverage the open and reinvent the clandestine and covert.

63. I will not belabor the failings of the USIC and the U.S. military intelligence community in "hiring to payroll," code for "fill as many desks as possible with the least expensive individuals;" nor will I harp on the reality that young people without significant overseas life experience are marginally qualified to be intelligence collectors, producers, or consumers. In this context, it is sufficient to observe that we have failed to champion quality education; we have failed to engage the other tribes of intelligence; and we have failed to provide for a reliable 24/7 network that can receive, make sense of, and exploit leads from citizens, be they domestic or foreign. The Israeli's excel at leveraging the global Jewish diaspora, and have a term for those who help the Mossad achieve clandestine objectives without qualm about betraying the government whose passport they carry: *sayonim*. See Gordon Thomas, *Robert Maxwell, Israel's Superspy: The Life and Murder of a Media Mogul*, Cambridge, MA: Da Capo Press, 2003.

64. In my view, universal service is the only possible foundation for truly achieving total assimilation of — and nationwide appreciation of and respect for — diversity. I do not believe individuals should be forced to join the Armed Services or to serve overseas, so my proposal distinguishes between a common bonding and training experience (2 months of common universal training including survivalist basics), followed by service in the Armed Forces or Peace Corps (voluntary), or in homeland service (mandatory). Such universal service — including mid-career universal service for immigrants — will establish a foundation upon which a University of the Republic can build cadres of human minds spanning all eight tribes that will network over a lifetime, and be the backbone for the smart nation.

65. See "Africa Cell Phone Provider's Ingenuity Turns to Wind and Solar," *EcoWorldly*, May 28, 2008.

66. See "Wireless Power Harvesting for Cell Phones," Duncan Graham-Rowe, *MIT Technology Review*, Tuesday, June 9, 2009.

67. A table of mobile SMS applications, nine pages as of May 2, 2009, is available from Earth Intelligence Network (EIN) in the Peace Book section (*www.oss.net/Peace*). It will be updated over time. Mr. Jason ("JZ") Liszkiewicz, Executive Director of EIN, is the editor and subject matter expert in this arena.

68. Statistical sources vary in the depiction of illiteracy among Muslim youth from country to country (and between urban and rural areas) but as a rule of thumb, at least one-third of these young Muslims are both illiterate and largely unemployed. There are not enough guns on the planet to kill them all — educating them to the point that they can create localized stabilizing wealth for themselves would appear to be the only sound strategic choice, as well as the only affordable and achievable choice.

69. A useful overview by Major Lynda Liddy, AU, is provided in "The Strategic Corporal: Some Requirements in Training and Education," *Australian Army Journal*, Vol. II, No. 2, Autumn 2005.

70. See "The Strategic Corporal: Leadership in the Three Block War," *Marines Magazine,* January 1999. The reality is that the USG does not train strategic corporals in any branch of the government with the possible exception of the U.S. Marines. We train clerks to do rote tasks, and we have too many chiefs that cannot do the job while our entire middle will be departing before 2012. *Now* is the time to redefine HUMINT as a national priority, but with full respect for all thirteen slices managed *together*. See the next note for the key to reinventing HUMINT with speed.

71. See *Field Manual (FM) 1, Warfighting* (USMC, 1989), Chapter 4. I quote this section in its entirety because this is precisely what the HUMINT discipline needs across all 13 slices:

> We achieve this harmonious initiative in large part through the use of the commander's intent. There are two parts to a mission: the task to be accomplished and the reason, or intent. The task describes the action to be taken while the intent describes the desired result of the action. Of the two, the intent is predominant. While a situation may change, making the task obsolete, the intent is more permanent and continues to guide our actions. Understanding our commander's intent allows us to exercise initiative in harmony with the commander's desires.
>
> In order to maintain our focus on the enemy, we should try to express intent in terms of the enemy. The intent should answer the question: What do I want to do to the enemy? This may not be possible in all cases, but it is true in the vast majority. The intent should convey the commander's vision. It is not satisfactory for the intent to be "to defeat the enemy." To win is always our ultimate goal, so an intent like this conveys nothing.
>
> From this discussion, it is obvious that a clear explanation and understanding of intent is absolutely essential to unity of effort. It should be a part of any mission. The burden of understanding falls on senior

and subordinate alike. The senior must make perfectly clear the result he expects, but in such a way that does not inhibit initiative. Subordinates must have a clear understanding of what their commander is thinking. Further, they should understand the intent of the commander two levels up. In other words, a platoon commander should know the intent of his battalion commander, or a battalion commander the intent of his division commander.

72. The contrast between the Eastern way of war emphasizing human intelligence and stealth with a small logistics footprint, and the Western way of war that emphasizes very expensive technical mass with a very big logistics footprint, is ably made by H. John Poole in such books as *The Tiger's Way: A U.S. Private's Best Chance for Survival*, Chevy Chase, MD: Posterity Press, 2003; and *Tactics of the Crescent Moon: Militant Muslim Combat Methods*, Chevy Chase, MD: Posterity Press, 2004.

73. This was first made known to me at the Peacekeeping Intelligence conference in Stockholm in December 2004. My trip report, for that specific gathering, and other relevant documents are easily viewed at *www.oss.net/Peace*.

74. Learn more at *www.strongangel3.net*. This endeavor is funded by the Defense Advanced Projects Agency (DARPA) and is one of its most valuable, and least-costly, contributions to stabilization and reconstruction operations.

75. I believe there has been considerable progress, to include patrols armed with video cameras, small unit UAVs, and other esoteric technologies, but we still have not figured out that we can recharge our batteries with foot-power on the march—see, to provide just one example, "Charging Your Mobile Phone Just By Walking." *Softpedia*, February 8, 2008. As this monograph went to security review, the U.S. Army's plans to issue multipurpose iPod Touch devices appeared in the press. See "Apple's New Weapon: To help Soldiers make sense of data from drones, satellites, and ground sensors, the U.S. military now issues the iPod Touch," *Newsweek*, April 27, 2009. If the U.S. Army made this a two-way tool, using Soldiers as sensors reporting via RapidSMS

as pioneered by UNICEF, then Civil Affairs patrols could call in "Peace Targets" and create an automated Stabilization and Construction "roadmap" for the area.

76. On July 10, 2009, the inspectors general from five federal agencies—the Justice Department, the DoD, the CIA, the National Security Agency, and the Office of the Director of National Intelligence—released an unclassified report investigating the origins and operations of the Bush administration's warrantless surveillance program. In the last couple of years, the DoD has been helping other countries appreciate the beneficial role of the IG at all levels, and there have been a couple of multinational IG conferences inspired by conferences of government auditors, but all are still working at the industrial level of not questioning fundamental systemic attributes as called for by the following: "To ensure continued stability and protect the economic gains of both developed and developing countries, we need to consider deep and systemic reforms based on an inclusive multilateralism for a global financial system that can better meet the challenges of the 21st century." Statement on the global financial crisis by the UN Secretary-General, November 2008.

77. A long-standing quote to this effect is, "Everybody who's a real practitioner, and I'm sure you're not all naïve in this regard, realizes that there are two uses to which security classification is put: the legitimate desire to protect secrets, and the protection of bureaucratic turf. As a practitioner of the real world, it's about 90% bureaucratic turf; 10% legitimate protection of secrets as far as I am concerned," Rodney McDaniel, then Executive Secretary of the National Security Council, to a Harvard University seminar, as cited in Thomas P. Croakley, ed., *C3I: Issues of Command and Control*, Washington, DC: National Defense University, 1991, p. 68.

78. General Zinni's observation is extremely relevant to our urgent needs, but neither the White House nor any major national security element is yet serious about creating the Strategy Center such as he envisions. Were the Open Source Agency (OSA) to be funded, the Strategy Center would be a part of it, and General Zinni is the most qualified candidate to manage it, while also managing a close relationship with the Multinational Decision Support Center in Tampa, FL. I would recommend the Danish

three-star previously there and who is now the senior Danish defense attaché in Washington, DC, to command the center.

79. The latest is "hair trace" as a means of validating or investigating recent travels and lifestyle habits of individuals under scrutiny. See "Hair test reveals travel, lifestyle," in *cnetnews*, *Military Tech*, Vol. 1, June 1, 2009.

80. We still do not do multinational security collaboration that would offer enormous dividends when we get around to it. In any given foreign capital for example, the Regional Security Officers (RSO) speak among themselves, but their video surveillance systems, their watch lists, and other technical and human measures are not integrated among embassies, and even less so with corporate general managers, NGO security networks, etc.

81. As stated by a recently returned J-2 from Afghanistan, speaking at the Swedish training course on "Information and Intelligence Cooperation in Multifunctional International Operations," Folke Bernadotte Academy, March 30-April 7, 2009. Notes and most of the briefings are available from *www.oss.net/Peace*.

82. NRT (Near-Real-Time) using *www.telelanguage.com* and other means including encrypted cellular telephones; SME (Subject-Matter Expert).

83. Intelink-U, which is not to be confused with the OSC, is now open to 11 nations, up from the long-standing seven nations. This is simply not serious, but it is understandable because Intelink-U is trapped inside a system-high mind-set and a system-high architecture. The fastest way to unscrew this and go totally multinational is to implement my concept for a Multinational Decision Support Center (MDSC) in Tampa, FL, that is also a two-way reach-back hub for each of 90+ nations.

84. If HUMINT were managed as I propose, senior management would quickly realize the benefits of redirecting excess funds from a clandestine cadre that cannot recruit as it should, to analysts able to legally commission works of very high value. Furthermore, if we follow the Dutch example of not going after anything with classified resources that can be gotten via OSINT,

we make our clandestine HUMINT 10 to 100 times more effective.

85. "Inherently governmental" is a vital phrase. I believe that individuals who leave government prior to retirement to accept offers from contractors should lose their clearances, which are a privilege attendant to their prior employment. Special Forces have the same problem. I consider both professions to be so demanding of integrity as to require a lifetime commitment. Second only to our overinvestment in technologies as a major misstep, is our over-reliance on contractors — 70 percent of the USIC budget, and increasing portions of the military services and civilian agencies, to the point that our government is less and less effective at higher and higher cost.

86. My second graduate thesis, at *Phi Beta Iota*, examines three embassies from an IO point of view, and concludes that most embassies access less than 20 percent of the relevant information, spilling 80 percent of that in the way they transfer it back to Washington, DC. Apart from being outnumbered by everyone else, the diplomats have no money with which to purchase OSINT, and the civilian spies, who have way too much money to throw around, insist on dealing only with traitors. I continue to believe that official cover should be an oxymoron, and the interagency analytic units should occupy every secure compartmented information facility (SCIF) in every embassy. This view is consistent with the recommendations made in the 1990s by Brigadier General Stewart with respect to installing interagency tactical analysis teams within each country team.

87. Two superb books for understanding the reality of OOTW are Bob Oakley, Michael Dziedzic, and Eliot Goldberg, *Policing the New World Disorder: Peace Operations and Public Security*, La Vergne, TN: University Press of the Pacific, 2002; and William Shawcross, *Deliver Us from Evil: Peacekeepers, Warlords and a World of Endless Conflict*, New York: Simon & Schuster, 2001. There is an entire literature on intelligence-led policing that DoD needs to master, along with the insight that law enforcement intelligence must be fully integrated into both CI and HUMINT elements at the planning stage, throughout operations, and staying over for a transition as indigenous security organizations assume responsibility.

88. Human Terrain System (HTS), available from *humanter-rainsystem.army.mil/default.htm*.

89. TRADOC had similar difficulties with respect to OSINT, ultimately creating a very shallow doctrinal approach that institutionalizes the various existing bits and pieces without actually pressing forward to define the total potential of OSINT done right. Apart from my belief that the time has come to restore a role for the individual branches (e.g., Army intelligence) in creating their own training and doctrine, I would venture to suggest that the time has also come to create a multinational concepts, doctrine, training, and collaboration network in which we can leverage the socio-economic, ideo-cultural, techno-demographic, and natural-geographic knowledge of all eight tribes of intelligence irrespective of nationality.

90. Project Camelot by the CIA in Latin America, and Project Grandview by the National Ground Intelligence Center (NGIC) are examples of prior endeavors. There are many others.

91. Two especially satisfying books on this strategic topic (apart from the ethnocentric literature) are Robert J. Gonzalez, ed., *Anthropologists in the Public Sphere: Speaking Out on War, Peace, and American Power*, Austin: University of Texas, 2004; and the classic by Ada Bozeman, *Strategic Intelligence & Statecraft: Selected Essays*, Dulles, VA: Brassey's, 1992. Here in its entirety is my brief review of the latter book, as it makes crystal clear why HTT cannot be successful apart from the other 15 slices of HUMINT.

> While reading this book, every intelligence professional should feel like a bashful second-grader shuffling their feet while being kindly reprimanded by their teacher. This book, a collection of essays from the 1980s, is the only one I have ever found that truly grasps the strategic long-term importance of intelligence in the context of culture and general knowledge. The heart of the book is on page 177: "(There is a need) to recognize that just as the essence of knowledge is not as split up into academic disciplines as it is in our academic universe, so can intelligence not be set apart from statecraft and society,

or subdivided into elements . . . such as analysis and estimates, counterintelligence, clandestine collection, covert action, and so forth. Rather, and as suggested earlier in this essay, intelligence is a scheme of entire things. And, since it permeates thought and life throughout society, Western scholars must understand all aspects of a state's culture before they can assess statecraft and intelligence." The 25-page introduction, at least, should be read by every intelligence professional.

92. See Wikipedia's Human Terrain System (HTS) and Human Terrain Team (HTT) pages for a shallow discussion of the controversies. Denounced by the American Anthropological Association and clearly incapable of fielding a sufficiency of either expertise or numbers, this program has nevertheless received $40 million from the Secretary of Defense, no doubt because his information about the program has been filtered and he is unaware of the documented and viscerally-deep criticisms of both the program manager and virtually every aspect of the program. A few minor successes aside (OSS created the tribal maps for both Afghanistan and Iraq that were given to Special Operations teams going in at a time when the CIA had no tribal maps), this program is the poster child for consolidating the HUMINT (and OSINT) program across all of the DoD and eventually the whole of government—in other words, the DoD needs to follow the advice of Colonel Vincent Stewart, USMC, then the OSINT Program Analyst for USD(I), and create the Defense Open Source Program (DSOP) and fully-fund the Open Source Agency (OSA) but under diplomatic auspices. HTT done right can be priceless.

93. As described in *Intelligence Operations and Metrics in Iraq and Afghanistan*, Washington, DC: RAND, November 2008.

94. I was first made aware of this point by a Postgraduate Intelligence Program (PGIP) thesis. I remember being very impressed. While standard to doctrine (See FM 7-98, Chap. 6 – Command, Control, Communications, and *Intelligence)*, it is especially important here.

95. See the excellent Wikipedia article on "Six Degrees of Separation," which taught me that Stanley Milgram's "Small World

Problem" was preceded by *Contacts and Influences* by Ithiel de Sola Pool and his student, Manfred Kochen. Finding a path from a known asset or personality to a desired asset or personality is a very important part of clandestine tradecraft as well as social networking, but more often than not is neglected by case officers in favor of random opportunism.

96. Ben de Jong, Wies Platje, and Robert Steele, eds., *PEACE-KEEPING INTELLIGENCE: Emerging Concepts for the Future*, Oakton, VA: OSS, 2003, both quotations, p. 92. Chapter 7 comprises pp. 73-100. In 2002, it was my very good fortune to be invited to speak on OSINT at a Dutch conference on Peacekeeping and Intelligence co-sponsored by the Netherlands Defence College (Institu Defensie Leergangen [IDL]) and the Netherlands Intelligence Studies Association (NISA). This conference, held on November 15-16, 2002, was my introduction to both the stars of peacekeeping intelligence, notably Major General Patrick Cammaert, RN NL, and Colonel Jan-Inge Svensson, Land Forces SE. Both remain devoted to creating the craft of peacekeeping intelligence (PKI). The very best of the speakers as well as the very best of those studying peacekeeping intelligence in the past, such as Professor Walter Dorn of Canada and Professor Hugh Smith of Australia are featured in the book.

97. There is a strong need for cohesive HUMINT management between this particular "slice," and the covert action and clandestine operations slices. I am mindful of and most respectful of the accomplishments of the United Kingdom (UK) 14 Intelligence Company, the SAS over-all, and the more recently commissioned Special Reconnaissance Regiment, and the UK Army Force Research Unit (FRU). I believe we can learn from others, but I also believe the USA can take the lead in coherent HUMINT. Richard Aldrich, *The Hidden Hand: Britain, America, and Cold War Secret Intelligence*, London, UK: Overlook Hardcover, 2002.

98. *Ibid.* A lengthy treatment of Bosnia, with previously unheard of academic access to all relevant classified files, is provided by Cees Wiebes, *Intelligence and the War in Bosnia, 1992-1995*, Amsterdam, Netherlands: Lit Verlag, 2003.

99. Processing, and especially near-real-time processing, remains the choke point. While spending trillions on secret collec-

tion the USIC has consistently neglected processing, to the point that today we still process less than 10 percent of all the signals we collect, and perhaps, given the rise in traffic, less than 5 percent. We do not have broad aggregate machine-speed pattern and anomaly detection at the strategic, operational, and tactical levels. Little has changed since my first book in 2000.

100. I specifically eschew any discussion of defensive counterespionage (DCE) or offensive counterespionage (OFCO).

101. I like the cryptic summary description by Joel Brenner, until recently the top USIC official for counterintelligence: "If there's a hole in your fence, security's job is to fix it. Our job in part is to figure out how it got there, who's been coming through it, and what they took when they left," he said, adding, "and how to return the favor." The first is defensive, the latter offensive counterintelligence. As quoted in Pamela Hess, "US counterintel chief to be replaced," Associated Press, June 26, 2009.

102. President Reagan blew NSA coverage of Libyan communications in relation to the Belle discotheque in West Berlin. The then director of the NSA is described as livid, but impotent. See David Wise, "Yakety-Yak: Assessing the Threat," *Los Angeles Times*, May 26, 2002. I have long believed that Presidents and other senior elected and appointed officers should not be beyond penalty for such disclosures, *and* that no President should be allowed to pardon one of their own staff for high crimes and misdemeanors whether directed by the President or not. We are long overdue for a massive reduction of secrecy and a draconian increase in the penalties for disclosing truly precious secrets.

103. Available from *www.freerepublic.com/focus/f-news/1543933/posts*.

104. The opposite of "can do no wrong" is the severe abuse of authority in conducting witch hunts and using power to terminate clearances without due process. Completely apart from the security clearance process being a total abject disaster, the use by management of "Fitness for Duty Physicals" (CIA) and arbitrary command-based revocation of access or clearances (two different things), is shameful.

105. Security Clearance Reform (SCR) has received attention, but is making little progress. Not only do good people get knocked out for truly insane reasons, but now we are told that one in four of those with clearances has serious derogatory information that was not noticed when clearances were granted. See "Pentagon Audit Finds Flaws In Clearances: One-fourth have 'derogatory' data," *The Washington Times*, June 4, 2009, p. 1.

106. Norman Polmar and Thomas Allen, *Merchants of Treason: America's Secrets for Sale,* New York: Dell, 1989.

107. Stuart Herrington, *Traitors Among US: Inside the Spycatcher's World*, Fort Washington, PA: Harvest Books, 2000. The two key lessons that jumped out at me were the importance of not allowing homesteading or long tours by classified material control specialists, particularly in and around Eastern Europe (at the time); and the equal importance of understanding the different cultural views on counterintelligence that are held by different categories of personnel, notably officers, warrant officers, noncommissioned officers with decades of service, and long-term civilian specialists.

108. In my own experience, the easiest traitors for the enemy to recruit are found in the ranks of the contracting community (70 percent of the secret budget, See Tim Shorrock, *Spies for Hire: The Secret World of Intelligence Outsourcing*, New York: Simon & Schuster, 2008). The Soviets are known to target contractors who have passed their lifestyle polygraph, and to run them until they are scheduled (rarely) for a follow-up polygraph, sometimes 12 years, if not longer. I recollect this tid-bit from, I believe, Christopher Andrew and Oleg Gordievsky, *Instructions from the Centre: Top Secret Files on KGB Foreign Operations, 1975-85*, London, UK: Hodder & Stoughton, 1993, but it might have been a later publication by the same authors. As a general rule, "false flag" approaches with a commercial flavor, i.e., "help me now, get a retirement job," are used by both national enemies, and the United States, as well as foreign contractors seeking an illegal advantage in pursuing budget share.

109. See "TAKEDOWN: Targets, Tools, & Technocracy," Ninth Annual Strategy Conference, U.S. Army War College,

Challenging the United States Symmetrically and Asymmetrically: Can America Be Defeated?" March 31-April 2, 1999, subsequently published in a book by the same title.

110. It is not my place to suggest changes in the strategic-tactical allocation of capabilities, but I do note with some interest that small programs are proliferating across the Services and commands, each generating its own practitioners with varying degrees of quality, capability, and authority. In today's world, the distinction has blurred between strategic and tactical capabilities, especially in the HUMINT arena, and I believe that there is much to be gained from a comprehensive review and a virtual integration that standardizes what can be standardized, while empowering the confederacy (everyone keeps their own armies) with a higher common efficacy.

111. Alfred Cumming, *Covert Action: Legislative Background and Possible Policy Questions*, Washington, DC: Congressional Research Service, February 9, 2009.

112. Radiological has been added in recent years because it is now known that entire cities can be made uninhabitable by the thoughtful spread of such materials. While nuclear in nature, a radiological weapon does not require a nuclear device or explosion for the spread of nuclear materials so as to severely contaminate an area. Such threats are overstated. Wrapping detonation cord around every crane in Long Beach Harbor is faster, better, cheaper, and will destroy shipping there for at least 2 weeks, a catastrophic economic blow. I believe we need to devise a multinational due process, perhaps modeled after the International Tribunal, so as to obtain balanced approval for actions that in my view should not be done unilaterally so as to avoid blow-back.

113. Sec. 503c of the National Security Act of 1947 [50 U.S.C. 413b] as cited by Cumming.

114. I include here the Safari Club, ill-advised U.S. funding of the Islamic radical wing of the Pakistani Inter-Services Intelligence (ISI) organization, and the covert or clandestine support for 41 of the 44 dictators now remaining, all of whom are "best pals" with the USG (the election of President Obama has changed

nothing) under the guise of collaborating in the Global War on Terrorism (GWOT). To be specific, we support personalistic dictatorships (20, now less Hussein in Iraq); monarch dictators (7, with Saudi Arabia being the first in class); military dictators (5, with U.S. allies Sudan and Pakistan being 1 and 2 respectively); communist dictators (5); dominant-party dictators (7); and lastly, theocratic dictators (1, Iran). Cuba, Iran, and North Korea are not our friends for ideological reasons largely unfounded in analytically-supported reason. This is discussed in Mark Palmer, *Breaking the Real Axis of Evil: How to Oust the World's Last Dictators by 2025*, New York: Rowman & Littlefield, 2005. Properly managed, national and military intelligence would not only define the "four forces after next" including the Peace Force, they would define the need for both an Undersecretary of Defense for Peace in the DoD, and an Undersecretary of State for Diplomacy in the Department of State, with two Assistant Secretaries: one for the dictators that agree to a 5 to 7-year exit strategy, and one for those that refuse.

115. Cumming; also, see Endnote 111.

116. The actual number appears in different sources as being from 12 to 21. See Greg Miller, "CIA's Ambitious Spy Plan Falters," *Los Angeles Times*, February 16, 2008. The reality is that the CIA knows nothing of the real-world and is now incapable of creating deep cover on a large scale. The only sustainable cover in today's era of digital records is one that is bona fide and has been created unwittingly by an individual acting legitimately (or illegitimately in the case of a Muslim merchant in Latin America, to take one example of a high-value potential recruitment) for at least a decade. To be truly effective at clandestine operations, we need to hire individuals with their existing cover identity, not in isolation for immersion in a totally flawed culture that lives immunity rather than cover.

117. The CIA's nominal executive agency for HUMINT not withstanding, it is now clear that Leon Panetta, who offered enormous potential for a renaissance of HUMINT, has been captured by the *status quo ante* crowd in both operations and analysis, and I do not see the CIA being a major player in either respect in the near to mid-term. As noted below, it may be best to redirect the CIA—and the director of the CIA—to better integrate technical collection requirements and evaluations.

118. I left the CIA at a time when the lawyer had replaced the bodyguard as the status symbol, and in my subsequent years of civilian military experience, I have learned that most military lawyers do not really know the law—and the applicable classified findings—as well as they should. When lawyers below the national command level say "you cannot do that," they usually mean "I don't really know for sure."

119. I am mindful of the extraordinary role played by the USD(I) today in orchestrating all elements of defense intelligence. As a long-time admirer of General James Clapper, USAF (Ret), I personally believe he is uniquely qualified to be the DNI, and that his eventual appointment as DNI could usefully be accompanied by a conversion of the USD(I) into a new Undersecretary of Defense for Operations Other Than War [USD(O)]. When he becomes the DNI, he can take the national agencies with him, and elevate the DIA to become the whole of government analytic arm. I continue to believe that the South-Central Campus should have three buildings, one each for education, intelligence, and research, while the existing new building for the DNI at Bolling AFB becomes a new all-source analytic facility, with the lower floors open to uncleared specialists doing OSINT in support of the all-source analysts across every domain.

120. A handful of special provisions could be included in the Smart Nation-Safe Nation Act to provide for truly secret operational capabilities. However, bureaucracies cannot keep secrets. The real challenge is to find leadership that is both fully capable of managing extraordinary operations that include the deliberate taking of life (one man-one bullet) and well-endowed with ethics. Ethics matter more when you are engaged in *sub-rosa* activities; they can be all that stands between a crime against humanity and a precision strike good for all. As discussed in the section on Covert Action, the law is either unclear or narrowly against active military covert operations; i.e., in theory, they can track a terrorist or drug lord, but not kill them. DoD-led multinational clandestine and covert activities are the fastest, best, and cheapest way to move ahead in the short-term, while we build longer-term capabilities that are completely nonofficial and very very good.

121. This was the effort to finally create a comprehensive collection management system across all classified disciplines, but as noted in the body of this monograph, it suffered from a complete lack of understanding among the so-called requirements and collection management specialists of OSINT, as well as multinational information-sharing and sense-making operations (both overt and covert).

122. Consumers who say "tell me everything about everything," or "you figure it out," have not been properly educated or trained. I lost my clearances to a system that could not fathom 7,500 legal, ethical foreign contacts. Finally, lawyers— (US-SOCOM) had to get a special ruling in 1997 from the Assistant Secretary of Defense for Intelligence Oversight to educate their Command's lawyers on the legality of acquiring open source information from U.S. citizens.

123. James Bamford, *Body of Secrets: Anatomy of the Ultra-Secret National Security Agency*, Prescott, AZ: Anchor, 2002, p. 613.

124. See "The Asymmetric Threat: Listening to the Debate," *Joint Force Quarterly*, Autumn/Winter 1998-1999; "Threats, Strategy, and Force Structure: An Alternative Paradigm for National Security in the 21st Century," *Strategic Alternatives Report,* Carlisle, PA: Strategic Studies Institute, November 2000; "Rebalancing the Instruments of National Power: The Forthcoming National Security Act of 2009," 2008; and most recently, "Fixing the White House and National Intelligence," OSS White Paper, April 2009; all four are available from *www.phibetaiota.net*.

125. Nunn; also, see Endnote 26.

126. Alfred M. Gray, "Intelligence Challenges in the 1990s," *American Intelligence Journal*, Winter 1989-1990. General Gray was then Commandant of the Marine Corps (CMC), and directed the establishment of the Marine Corps Intelligence Center (later renamed MCIA) as well as the Marine Corps University. He was an educator of the most extraordinary sort. This article by General Gray remains the single most intelligent piece of policy wisdom yet published, particularly with respect to the need for OSINT

about nonconventional threats, and the need to create unclassified intelligence justifying "peaceful preventive measures." In the right-hand column, (Asymmetric) and (e.g., Off the Shelf) have been added to this depiction; otherwise this is as originally published in 1989.

127. The summary of this 1998 conference was published as "The Asymmetric Threat: Listening to the Debate," *Joint Force Quarterly*, Autumn/Winter 1998-99.

128. A summary of the 2008 Army Strategy Conference, "Rebalancing the Instruments of National Power," is available from *www.phibetaiota.net/?p=15655*.

129. Creating the OSA under diplomatic auspices with non-reimbursable funding from the DoD creates everything we need to get a grip on all information in all languages all the time, and provides the multinational foundation for collaboration in the full spectrum of HUMINT from overt to covert, against all 10 high-level threats to humanity. Putting General Zinni in charge of the embedded national Strategy Center adds so much value that I speculate he would be identifying both huge costs savings across whole of government operations in direct support of the Director of OMB, at the same time that he would be providing the international community with a Global Range of Needs Table with which to orchestrate U.S. $1 trillion a year in combined financial and social investment by organizations, and peer-to-peer giving by individuals. *This is not rocket science. All it takes is one decision.*

130. My short memorandum on Chinese irregular warfare, available from *www.phibetaiota.net/?p=15866*, barely scratches the surface. They are exporting men, and clearly doing very well in the two areas where the United States is incapacitated: grand strategy, and whole of government campaign planning and operations. The only way we can have a win-win with the eight challengers (Brazil, China, India, Indonesia, Iran, Russia, Venezuela, and Wild Cards such as Congo, Malaysia, and Turkey) is if we fund the World Game and EarthGame as shared assets.

131. President Obama lacks access to Epoch B leaders that

understand bottom-up development. He is trapped in a bubble with industrial era carpetbaggers. From *Small is Beautiful: Economics As If People Mattered* to *Human Scale* to *ELECTION 2008: Lipstick on the Pig*, Oakton, VA: Earth Intelligence Network, 2008, the literature is clear. Spend money on individual Americans, and they will restore the Republic in terms of both infrastructure and morality. There is an entire literature on resilience, adaptability, and panarchy (the opposite of anarchy).

132. I served on the Information Handling Committee (IHC) of the U.S. Intelligence Community as a whole, and also on the Advanced Information Processing and Analysis Steering Group (AIPASG) of the IC-wide Research & Development Committee (R&DC). We found 20 different "all-source fusion" desktop projects, each funded by a different element of the IC (with multiples at the NSA and the CIA), all with different requirements, different individual contractors, and uniformly mediocre results. The IC has spent close to a trillion dollars on technical collection, and it still has no large-scale all-source fusion processing center, nor does any analyst anywhere—inclusive of "the pit" at USSCOM— have a proper digital desktop within which to exercise all 18 of the functionalities identified in the 1985 report, *Computer-Aided Tools for the Analysis of Science & Technology (CATALYST)*, Washington, DC: Central Intelligence Agency, October 1989. For a list of software used by J-23 USSOCOM, see my memorandum online, which also includes TOOZL elements and other notes, available from *www.phibetaiota.net/?p=10653,* undated memorandum.

133. I have studied Endeca, Palantir, the various CI/HUMINT tool sets and systems, and those initiatives of the Defense HUMINT Management Office (DMHO) that are described in the open source literature, e.g., "Defense HUMINT Needs Technology, Too," *SIGNAL Magazine*, October 2006. The most obvious short-fall I see is that DMHO is too heavily reliant on others and does not have direct access to the top U.S. IT scouts, such as Stephen Arnold, CEO of Arnold IT, the only person outside of Google that understands all of their patents, and the top person in the United States on visualization, social network mapping, anomaly detection, and other emergent IT capabilities that tend not to be noticed by the DoD. I gave up on In-Q-Tel a decade ago when my conference audience said it did not add value.

134. I described this requirement to an Israeli officer in the 1990s. He laughed and said "We have the solution." When I asked, he was quick to respond: "A dog on a 500-meter leash." They do not actually need leashes. While I hesitate to expand HUMINT to include trained dogs, I absolutely believe we have not done enough to leverage animal senses in MASINT or in support of HUMINT.

135. As of April 8, 2009 the Defense Information Systems Agency (DISA) was seeking help in finding Web 2.0 technologies; some are now at Web 4.0.

136. See my Annotated Bibliography at *www.oss.net/BOOKS*, or for more active browsing, use the Reviews section available at *www.phibetaiota.net*.

137. George Will, *Statecraft as Soulcraft*, New York: Touchstone, 1984.

138. In the past few years, I have spontaneously replicated some of the thinking that Buckminster Fuller did first, and have been much taken with the title of one of his books, *Only Integrity is Going to Count*, New York: Critical Path Publishing, Abridged Ed., March 2004. He describes us as information harvesters, and states that problems are rarely physical. In this, he is joined by Will Durant, who points out that social philosophy is the crux of all human behavior, and what we do there determines all else. So far, we are failing to achieve the ascendance of which we are capable. A structured look at his thinking is available from *www.designsciencelab.com*.

APPENDIX

ARMY STRATEGY CONFERENCE OF 2008

Elsewhere I provide 29 pages of detailed notes on this superb recent conference, as well as a 14-page article on the conference submitted to the *Joint Force Quarterly*.[1]

Here are the bare bone highlights from the 2008 conference:

- Challenges more complex, threats more dispersed.
- Super-empowered individuals and nontraditional social networks.
- Five D's must be carried out simultaneously:
  - Diplomacy
  - Defense
  - Development
  - Domestic capability (private sector mobilized by commerce)
  - Decision support (unclassified intelligence, harmonizing efforts).
- Preventive action, influence of others, and support to indigenous are key.
- Pearl Harbor had three long-term negative effects:
  - Military took over national security process.
  - Technical intelligence took over the budget.
  - We substituted technology for thinking," have a strategic deficit.
- Not exercising U.S. influence in an intelligent cost-effective manner.
- We are weakest in irregular warfare (waging peace).
- Security must be redefined—high-level threats respect no boundaries.

- USG handicapped in multiple ways:
  - Very little stability — constant churn in people and budgets.
  - Lack interagency culture of collaboration.
  - Lack flexible, sustainable, responsive budgets.
  - We can influence rather than command, bad at both.
  - We have a *huge* historical knowledge gap.
  - We have a *huge* cultural knowledge gap.
  - Human terrain program lacks resources.
  - Less than 1 percent of DoD budget spent on social sciences.[2]
  - New money pays for tools, not data[3]
  - There is no coordination of research across agencies or services.
  - Innovators are too low in the chain.
  - Bureaucratic turf wars continue to set us back, at home and overseas.
- Good News:
  - 2 4/7 reachback, when it is available, is deeply valued.
  - Human Terrain System (HTS) credited with reducing kinetic 60-70 percent.
  - After 9/11, NGOs more open to joint efforts.
  - 38,000 NGOs have substantial budgets and capabilities.
- Bad News:
  - DoD must give up major systems to fund peace operations.
  - We are being destroyed by adversary information operations (IO).
  - Simplest things are now virtually impossible (e.g., building a road fast).
  - Lack ability to field full range of expertise across all departments.

- Agencies and services continue to game the system, not collaborate.
- USG is a systemic failure — horizontal challenges, vertical organizations.
- We cannot answer question: what is being spent by all in one place?
- We have no integrators or strategic connectors in the USG.
- Indications and warnings are not coming from the secret side.
• We Need:
- Brutally honest roles and missions debate.
- Resident military advisors everywhere (not bases).
- Advisor Corps equivalent to 18th Airborne.
- Many more multinational students who could become leaders.
- Deep lasting relationships at every level in every country and organization.
- Ability to understand and leverage all actors.

I must stress that the above points are extracted from detailed notes of what was said by scores of speakers and participants within the 2008 conference and represent my personal interpretation of what was said to the assembled audience.[4]

ENDNOTES - APPENDIX

1. Both are available from *www.oss.net/Peace*, along with other raw references being put together for a new book, *PEACE INTELLIGENCE: Multinational Multifunctional Information-sharing and Sense-Making*, available in raw form from *www.phibetaiota. net/?p=6362*.

2. This is equivalent to the U.S. intelligence community and its treatment of "Open Sources," which receive less than 1/2 of 1 percent of all funding, even though an increase to 5 percent would increase by a factor of 10 to 1000 what we could know that is relevant to any given strategic intelligence target.

3. This is especially true in the geospatial arena, where announcements are made about the expenditures on open sources but where the reality is that 80 percent of the money is being spent on building bridges from legacy systems optimized for precision imagery, not wide-area surveillance, to modern commercial imagery systems, and there is virtually no money for either acquiring all Russian 1:50,000 combat charts for the 90 percent of the world for which we do not have combat charts with contour lines on the shelf, or for buying at least one pass of commercial imagery for every instability zone.

4. Complete citations with the notes are available from *www.oss.net/Peace*. Over 1,400 nonfiction book reviews helpful to achieving a global strategic perspective are available from *www.phibetaiota.net*.

U.S. ARMY WAR COLLEGE

Major General Robert M. Williams
Commandant

*****

STRATEGIC STUDIES INSTITUTE

Director
Professor Douglas C. Lovelace, Jr.

Director of Research
Dr. Antulio J. Echevarria II

Author
Mr. Robert D. Steele

Director of Publications
Dr. James G. Pierce

Publications Assistant
Ms. Rita A. Rummel

*****

Composition
Mrs. Jennifer E. Nevil

www.ingramcontent.com/pod-product-compliance
Lightning Source LLC
Chambersburg PA
CBHW081402270326
41930CB00015B/3383